The House to Ourselves

The House to Ourselves

Reinventing Home Once the Kids Are Grown

TODD LAWSON AND **TOM CONNOR**

PHOTOGRAPHS BY ROB KAROSIS

The Taunton Press

EDITOR: Marilyn Zelinsky Syarto

INTERIOR DESIGN: Dania Davey

LAYOUT: Dania Davey and Carol Petro

ILLUSTRATOR: Christine Erikson

PHOTOGRAPHER: Rob Karosis, except as noted above

The Taunton Press
Inspiration for hands-on living®

The Taunton Press, Inc., 63 South Main Street, PO Box 5506, Newtown, CT 06470-5506

e-mail: tp@taunton.com

Distributed by Publishers Group West

Library of Congress Cataloging-in-Publication Data

Lawson, Todd.
  The house to ourselves : reinventing home once the kids are grown /
Todd Lawson and Tom Connor.
    p. cm.
  ISBN 1-56158-490-8
  1. Empty nesters--Dwellings--United States. 2.
Dwellings--Remodeling--United States. I. Connor, Tom. II. Title.
NA7195.E56C66 2004
728'.37'0286--dc22

                        2003020635

Printed in Singapore
10 9 8 7 6 5 4 3 2 1

The following manufacturers/names appearing in *The House to Ourselves* are trademarks and/or registered trademarks: Cabot®, Porsche®, Sub-Zero®.

Acknowledgments

Architects and homeowners are frequently thanked near the end of the acknowledgments page in home design books. But, without them, this book would not exist, so we'll begin by thanking them.

We are especially grateful to the couples whose houses grace these pages. They were exceedingly gracious, welcoming us into their homes, treating us as guests and friends, and giving of themselves to extraordinary degrees. We also wish to thank the architects who designed these exceptional projects and who were generous with their time and insights. Each architect illuminated different aspects of *The House to Ourselves*.

At The Taunton Press, which produces the most beautiful design books published today, we would like to thank Steve Culpepper for the great idea, and Peter Chapman, Marilyn Zelinsky Syarto, Wendi Mijal, Paula Schlosser, Maria Taylor, publisher James Childs, and Robyn Aitken.

Special thanks are due to Rob Karosis, whose photographs capture the essence of empty-nester living, and to our families and friends for their patience and support.

—Todd Lawson and Tom Connor

Contents

Introduction

When we started writing this book, we set out to find homes designed to satisfy the needs of empty nesters, one of the fastest growing groups of Americans today. First, however, we had to look at the stereotypes frequently applied to baby boomers whose children have grown and left home. To some, the term "empty nester" might suggest someone who leads a life diminished of prospects for the future. To others, the term may define retirees who would typically migrate to Florida or move to traditional retirement communities.

As we got to know the architects and home-owners and visited the homes that are shown in this book, we began to see and marvel at the variety, invention, and creativity that are reflected in these empty-nester homes we've come to call "the house to ourselves."

"The house to ourselves" reflects a major new trend in home design. Driven in large part by the baby-boom generation, today's baby boomers possess brave new ideas about where and how they want to live. Location poses no barriers to today's empty nester. We visited a couple who moved to a

sunny, urban villa in Mexico, another who built a contemporary farmhouse on a wild meadow in Indiana, and a third baby-boomer couple who built a soaring addition of glass, stone, and steel in the shadows of the Grand Tetons in Wyoming. A number of other empty nesters realized their dream of living on the water in sophisticated and well-designed homes that are far from the sandy, delicate beach cottages of the past.

Although the houses we saw—wherever their location—were designed with couples in mind, these nests were far from empty. The majority of them were designed to accommodate visiting children, grand-children, and guests in imaginative ways.

Some owners built family compounds with companion buildings nearby to accommodate guests while keeping their master bedrooms separate and private.

One couple built their son a guesthouse on the property, elegantly buffered from the main house by a swale of greenery. In a renovated Rhode Island cottage, a walkway from the main house leads to a new two-story guesthouse for kids and grandkids. An island vacation/retirement retreat on the West Coast has room for the grandkids in a bunkroom at the opposite end of the house from the owners' master bedroom suite.

It is creative solutions such as these, we discovered, that are keeping the new empty-nester family separate but very much together during visits.

We met other baby boomers who wanted to stay in the home in which they raised their children, but in remodeling them to suit their new lives, the houses no longer resemble family-style homes. A 1960s Dutch Colonial in Connecticut

was transformed into a light-filled retreat with an open floor plan and additions for collections of art and antique clocks. A turn-of-the-century cottage in California was also transformed from dark, cramped and musty to spacious, airy and elegant. It amazed us to see how couples could remain in their old and familiar neighborhoods while moving so far away from their former lifestyles.

While a good number of houses were conceived as retirement homes, there's nothing "retiring" about any of them. We visited an apartment in a retirement community that was altered into an artist's loft by a couple who once taught and painted. But that was only one instance. Everywhere we went we found houses filled with vibrant, rejuvenating, and liberating designs that let these baby boomers lead the lives they have dreamt about for so long.

We hope that the ideas we gathered and the inspiration we experienced while writing this book will serve you as you set out on the adventure of finally having the house to yourselves.

The Joy of Having
The House To Ourselves

THE COZY COTTAGE was the perfect place to raise three children. They slept soundly in the small bedrooms and played house in the pantry, free to draw on the room's unpainted pine paneling. When the kids moved out of the house to raise families of their own, Jim and Denny Hoelter found themselves with lots of unusable room. The house they lived in for 30 years no longer served their needs as a couple.

Since Jim and Denny loved the house, even with all its strengths and weaknesses, they decided to stay and renovate rather than move. The Hoelters worked with an architect to ready their house for a brand-new style of living together as a couple.

The Hoelters represent a large generation of baby boomers seeking to celebrate their future lifestyles by reinventing the existing family house, building new, or moving to like-minded communities to suit their changing needs and interests.

The trend is significant. About 70 million people in the United States have hit the half-century mark. Design-savvy baby boomers are using their life experiences and knowledge of their deep-seated desires to rewrite the book on architecture after having their children and careers.

The couple who built this house in Seaside, Florida, was drawn to the town's cozy, charming atmosphere. They specifically designed their bedroom so that they could look out over the tops of neighboring houses to catch a glimpse of the blue waters of the Gulf of Mexico.

The addition of dormers helped to convert the attic of this turn-of-the-century cottage into a light-filled master bedroom. The dormers also carved out special spaces, such as this window seat, where visiting grandchildren gather for storytelling time.

This retreat, built of native stone and wood, shows how one empty-nester couple passionately planned their new house around the environment. They wanted their home to blend into, not overwhelm, the landscape.

After raising six children and pursuing two careers, the homeowners of this new house wanted to live life to the fullest and wanted their home to mirror their passions. The house is located in northern Montana, but a love of travel abroad and a passion for entertaining informed the design of this European-style home.

A Liberating Time

These new empty nesters are independent-minded individualists. Unlike many in their parents' generation, many baby boomers see their future as a continuation of adventure and learning. While they retire earlier than their parents did, they are more likely to continue to pursue passions, hobbies, and even new careers well into their sixties, seventies, and beyond. Because many were wise about saving money for retirement, they have greater disposable income for their next house. Traditionally, mature couples downsized to smaller quarters after raising children and pursuing careers. Or they stayed in the family home and made some minor changes; maybe a children's bedroom became a sewing room or a home office. Yet the basic floor plan remained unchanged, with small, enclosed spaces for cooking and dining and a handful of bedrooms upstairs.

People change, however, and so do houses. The new empty-nester houses are radically different from those of the past.

Earlier generations may have opted to move to traditional retirement homes or to warmer climates, but today's baby boomers are venturing into urban as well as rural areas across the country. They are also just as likely to remain in the areas in which they have raised families, to stay surrounded by the network of children, friends, and professional

■ Professional kitchens that are built in large, open spaces, such as the one in this new home in Montana, indulge the empty nester's passion for entertaining on a grand scale. Half-walls allow the cook to visit with guests.

acquaintances that took years to build. The houses in this book are devoted solely to the wants and needs of the current generation of empty nesters—men and women who have the opportunity to design or renovate a home for no one else but themselves. All of the houses are distinctly different in their form and floor plan from traditional empty-nester houses. Master-bedroom suites are frequently positioned on the first level for easy access, cooking and dining areas designed expressly for entertaining dominate the house, and entire wings devoted to home offices or studios fulfill lifelong artistic dreams or keep creative juices flowing.

New Living Choices

The decision to buy a family house typically revolves around family interests. Usually, it is a compromise between the school district and the commute to work; resale value is also a key consideration. Newly independent couples, however, no longer need to worry about prize school districts, short commutes, or curb appeal. What is important to them now is the quality of their current lives.

Independent couples know that they can not only have the house to themselves but also have it any way and anywhere they want. Their dream houses materialize in four ways: They renovate the family home, remodel an

The owners of this home used to live in a city town house, but always dreamed of moving to a remote area with lots of space and rolling hills. Today's design-savvy empty nesters appreciate large parcels of open land that can be cultivated into special settings.

grandchildren, the living choices their close friends have made, and whether or not they want to move to a favorite vacation spot that holds cherished memories.

Remodeling the Family Home

For some couples, it's hard to leave the traditional family home once the kids are gone. The house's choppy layout of cramped, separated rooms is a familiar place with close friends in the neighborhood and doctors, banks, and clubs a few miles away. But there are as many possibilities in remodeling the family house as there are in designing a new home. Recasting the existing floor plan and redefining interior spaces are ways to make a family home work as a house for a couple.

One couple in Connecticut did just that. They worked with architect Craig Saunders to turn a standard,

existing home in another neighborhood, design and build a new house, or retire to a community with fellow baby boomers.

To make this important decision, couples often weigh in on the location of their grown children and

On a rolling tract of former farmland in rural Indiana, with no neighbors in sight, who needs privacy blinds in the master bath? Unfettered views like this, and the freedom to be as you are in your own home, appeal to the baby-boom generation.

This well-designed home is located on an island with an abundance of wild, native grasses. Even in casual environments, today's empty nesters feel free to express their sophistication and style when building a house.

builders' Colonial floor plan into an open and flowing showcase for their art and antique clock collections (see "Time for a Change" on p.174). Once the children were out of the house, the homeowners were also free to use the existing space for other activities, such as designing furniture. The homeowners also wanted to take advantage of the views of their landscape and added 700 square feet to the house to achieve their dream. Bedroom balconies open into a glassed-in tower and first-floor spaces. A soaring, two-story sunroom leads to terraces and gardens. A bowed deck wraps around two sides of the house like the prow of a ship.

The experience of transforming this couple's family home was like designing a new house but without ever having to leave the block.

Moving Up

Some baby boomers plan to leave their familiar neighborhood for a home that is dramatically different from their beloved family house. Builders, architects, and real-estate agents categorize this long-cresting wave of empty-nester homebuyers as a "move-up market," and these buyers are seeking design characteristics they have lived without while living in the family house.

While three basic principles drove the design of the family

LOW-MAINTENANCE LANDSCAPES

Empty-nester couples prefer smaller, contained yards that require less maintenance. As a result, outdoor spaces that once were covered in grass for children to play on are frequently being transformed into exotic courtyards of gardens, stone, and water.

In Brentwood, California, homeowners Suzi and Steve Gilbert enclosed a large corner lot to create four small, easy-to-maintain courtyards enclosing a graveled entry court, flower beds, and a pool (see "Refining the Ranch" on p. 88).

At the same time, a large yard can be easy to maintain. John and Cynthia Ruhaak raised two children in a suburban town house with no private property. Now, John takes 20 minutes to mow a central, grassed courtyard. There is no hint of concrete, however. An enclosed courtyard off their kitchen and dining room is all gravel for minimal upkeep and, beyond its walls, are 9 acres of wild Indiana meadowland that never needs maintenance.

■ The design of this walled yard makes the space inviting. The walls are high enough for privacy yet low enough so they won't block neighbors' views. Low-maintenance gravel replaces a grass yard.

■ In a California retirement community inhabited by longtime friends, life is playful and loosely structured. As with other buildings in the community, the exterior siding of this single bedroom and library tower are color coded according to function as well as for visual appeal. The communal spaces have siding painted yellow while private rooms have siding painted red.

house—practical, economical, and functional—fantasy and flight of the imagination drives the design of the independent couple's home. They have the discretionary income to find the space they want—whether it is an existing house with 14-foot-high ceilings, a kitchen with an eight-burner professional cooktop, or a hot tub hidden in the garage. Though we have heard much about baby boomers looking to downsize, many are actually moving into larger, custom-designed houses.

Whether it is planning a renovation of an existing home or designing a new home, baby boomers expect to have a voice in every aspect of the process. As a result, single-family home developers and retirement communities now offer more design and color-palette options than in the past. Builders are also offering more of the types of spaces and features this generation says it wants, such as putting master-bedroom suites on the first floor.

Designing a New Home

Baby boomers are also spending their discretionary income on designing and building new houses located closer to relatives and grown children. Others build far from civi-

A communal living room that looks this welcoming isn't likely to be found in a traditional retirement home. Having "the house to ourselves" doesn't just mean living in isolation; it also means baby boomers are living with whom they want, the way they want.

■ Empty-nester houses do away with walls to create a flowing, open plan. But they can also be divided up when the space is too large or when guests need their privacy. Here, the sliding door separates the two parts of the house so homeowners and visitors have visual and acoustical privacy.

lization because they crave the privacy of having a house to themselves, whether on an island or in the middle of the woods.

Couples who design a new house are fully involved in the process and are able to use their life experience to create a home that expresses their tastes. At this stage in their lives, they know themselves well. And they know from vacationing in different

parts of the world where they want to live. They have both vacationed together as a family and separately from the family and know what works best for them. Some share a place with other couples year after year to see if they can all live together upon retirement as an informal community. Others seek out a house in a like-minded community.

Communities of Fellow Empty Nesters

Baby boomers who love the idea of living in a community usually prefer one that allows for freedom of expression. The traditional, formal retirement communities—with rules, restrictions, and set design packages—can feel too restrictive to today's active couples. The developers and builders of planned retirement communities are sitting up and taking notice of this emerging generation of empty nesters. We are beginning to see well-designed units with more design choices in atypical retirement regions such as the Midwest and the Northeast.

Planned retirement communities are springing up in the most unlikely places. In southern California, a couple of retired teachers bought into an apartment complex associated with the University of California at Davis (see "A Hip Retirement Haven" on p. 24). Before moving in, the couple hired Cheng Design to redesign the basic floor plan of a standard one-bedroom unit in The University Retirement Community, a new type of neighborhood serving a generation of baby boomers who value learning at any age. Similar communities associated with colleges and universities are springing up elsewhere across the country—in Ames, Iowa, for example, and in Collegeville, Minnesota.

■ Empty nesters often design new houses using native materials and regional architectural preferences as a way to honor the authenticity of the site in which they choose to live. Although this Texas house is new, the locally milled cedar poles and limestone walls help the home resemble antique barn and utility structures found around the area.

■ Emphasizing the empty nester's interest in style and sophisticated materials, oversize Italian porcelain tiles balance and lighten the natural tone of the custom-designed vanity, which is handmade from Douglas fir and a polished concrete countertop.

Groups of unconventional baby boomers are also bypassing formal planned communities to create their own, more casual retirement neighborhood. A group of longtime friends decided to live together in a compound made up of public and private spaces they call "Cheesecake" (see "In the Company of Friends" on p. 40).

The locations where baby boomers choose to live today vary greatly from the way retirees traditionally sought refuge. In tandem with the freedom of locations comes the freedom of building individualized homes. Though each house in this book is distinctive from one another, all of the houses have something in common, namely the six design characteristics that make up the empty-nester home.

Designing It Our Way

Though the living choices are varied, there are five design concepts that are essential to this emerging type of house: single-level living; an open floor plan; flexible, accessible space; specialty rooms; and quality materials and craftsmanship. In addition, the sixth concept, low-maintenance landscape, is a key exterior feature. These characteristics comprise the basic building blocks that guide the design of the new empty-nester house.

SINGLE-LEVEL LIVING eliminates the second and third floors to allow a couple to live comfortably together with little distance and few walls between them. A single-level, open floor plan usually includes one large, central social space—which

■ In its former incarnation as a 1940s ranch-style house, rooms were closed off from one another, isolating them from the rest of the house. By widening and realigning doorways, rooms now flow easily into one another, creating an open floor plan with long vistas.

includes the kitchen and dining and living areas—with other smaller, more private spaces located off this central area.

The organization of single-level living also allows master bedrooms to be well separated from guest quarters on the same floor. In designing a vacation/retirement home for a couple on San Juan Island off the coast of Washington State, architect Geoffrey Prentiss positioned the master suite—bedroom, bath, and office—at one end of the central great room (see "A Couple's Island Lodge" on p. 78). At the opposite end of the floor, beyond the kitchen and dining area, is a guest wing with bedrooms and bunk house for their grown daughters and the couple's grandchildren. The arrangement not only gives each generation its own space but also ensures easy accessibility—now and in the future—for the couple.

AN OPEN FLOOR PLAN is a common characteristic of an empty-nest house design. With fewer family members living in the house, there is less need for walls for visual and acoustical separation. A new house designed with an open layout allows the floor plan to expand and contract as needed, to accommodate guests, or so couples can experience intimate spaces within common areas. To accomplish this flexibility in an open plan, sliding doors that close off entire wings or just a hallway are designed in many of the houses in this book. The doors are opened when guests arrive and closed off for privacy when guests sleep; or when

The current baby-boom generation won't let tradition stand in the way of a new experience. For a house on the beach in Washington State, a feat of engineering omits obstructions such as corner posts, letting the dining room seemingly float out onto a second-story deck and the horizon.

High-quality materials and superior hand-craftsmanship define today's empty-nester house. Here, on San Juan Island, off the coast of Washington State, carpenters trained as shipwrights built a handsome stairway out of vertical-grain Douglas fir.

the house is occupied by just two people, the doors enclose them in a private, cozy enclave.

THE CONCEPT OF FLEXIBLE SPACE is important to couples whose children and grandchildren frequently visit. Flexibility means that guest spaces can have other uses as well. Additionally, architects are placing guest and in-law rooms close to master bedrooms so that overnight or live-in help will be close by.

ACCESSIBILITY becomes more important as baby boomers' lives evolve. They need to plan for the time when they will need a home designed with accessibility in mind. Architects are taking into consideration design features such as well-designed ramps, wider hallways and doorways for wheelchair access, lower kitchen counters, and roll-in showers. A number of empty-nester houses are being built with an elevator—or at least the space for one when and if the homeowner needs it in the future.

SPECIALTY ROOMS—such as gourmet kitchens, wine cellars, media rooms, game rooms, and greenhouses—are popular features in the baby-boomer house, as couples pursue their passions more frequently and fervently once kids and careers

are behind them. According to architects and builders interviewed for this book, the most requested room by empty nesters and retirees is still the central great room, used for entertaining. The popularity of the great room grew out of this generation's love of family and fun. Whether the room is grand or modest in scale, it has an

A family compound of buildings lets empty-nester homeowners have their privacy while sharing their homes with grown children and visitors. The owners of this home had so many guests, they needed to spread out over two acres of waterfront property.

open and easy flow into adjoining spaces on the main living level.

Home offices and his-and-her studios and workshops are the next most popular spaces in the couple's new house. For a good number of baby boomers, their relationship to work and career will continue onward, even if it is in a reduced capacity.

Couples are going beyond turning the spare bedroom into a computer or sewing room. They are designing large personalized spaces or separate buildings for working, painting, weaving, fiddling, or thinking. Judith, for example, used to weave in a dark back bedroom off the kitchen. Now, her two-story studio is given prominence in both her life and in the design of her new home (see "A Weaver and Woodcutter's Refuge" on p. 182).

THE QUALITY OF MATERIALS AND CRAFTSMANSHIP is an important design element for empty nesters. Whether designing a renovated or new house, baby boomers want the value and comfort of living with natural, solid materials. Granite counters replace the practical laminate surfaces of family houses. Antique-wood floorboards add elegance to former vinyl kitchen floors of an existing neighborhood house.

In Jamestown, Rhode Island, the owners of a 1930s beach house renovated the weekend retreat by upgrading the materials used on the interior and exterior walls, floors, and ceilings (see "An Old Cottage Made New" on p. 108). Refurbished old brick, clear-varnished maple floors, and vertical tongue-and-groove wall panels painted white transformed a dingy coastal cottage into a bright and inviting beach house.

Creating a House for Yourself

The houses in this book show you how the homeowners used design concepts, features, and details to create a house for themselves. You'll discover ways to incorporate your wants, needs, and desires into a new home crafted to speak to your individual passions. Though some of the homeowners chose to make room for visiting family members, the intent of the new empty-nester house is to create the kind of space couples need to pursue unfettered comfort, happiness, and lives full of zeal.

The 21 empty-nester houses featured in this book naturally fall into four main sections according to homeowners' options, intentions, and pursuits. Each story includes the decisions behind the homeowners' individual choices.

The first part, called "Finding Our Place," explores the range of possibilities open to today's empty

Balconies off the master bedrooms expand private spaces while at the same time nurturing the empty nesters' love of living outdoors.

nesters: staying in the neighborhood or moving away to the city or country; and renovating, building a new larger or smaller house, or joining homes with friends and others from their generation. The second section, called "Just the Two of Us," features houses devoted to independent couples who have decided to live at home together, with no one else in the house. A third part, entitled "Separate but Together," looks at the creative ways in which parents can

have the nest to themselves and still share it with visiting children, grandchildren, and friends. Finally, the last part, "Pursuing Our Passions," highlights homes designed around the interests, hobbies, and obsessions couples are finally able to explore once they have the dedicated space—whether it's one room or the entire house.

The House to Ourselves is a book brimming with inspirational ideas for the new empty-nester home.

Each house featured in the book exemplifies the best designs for the grown-up dreams we all hold near and dear to our hearts. The homeowners and architects talk about the challenges they faced and the fresh solutions they found to help them create their ideal home. Each story answers these complex questions: Where will we live and what will our home look like now that we finally have the house all to ourselves?

▌ Empty nesters appreciate intricately designed indoor/outdoor spaces, such as courtyards. This courtyard is designed around a 200-year-old tree with a floor paved with smooth river stones.

Many baby boomers, like the couple who moved to this compound on the coast of Martha's Vineyard, take to the water, drawn to its serenity and the timeless ebb and flow of the ocean. This view is from a second-floor terrace off the master bedroom in the main cottage.

PART ONE

Finding Our Place

The Next House as Pure Possibility

A HIP RETIREMENT HAVEN

Davis, California

APARTMENTS IN A TYPICAL RETIREMENT COMMUNITY often have standardized floor plans, materials, and color palettes. But John and Polly, a retired teacher and artist, moved to California's University Retirement Community and discovered that they could have the security of kinship they desired while living in a distinctive, well-designed apartment that differed from the stock floor plan and design package. All it took was a little ingenuity and some innovative interior designs from a pair of architects to push their ideas through the apartment complex's building developers.

After years of rambling around in a six-story contemporary house, John and Polly decided they needed fewer levels to live comfortably. They bought a 1,200-square-foot apartment in the retirement community before the ground was broken. They knew that each of the 400 apartment units would have window trellises, quaint balconies, white railings, and small, tidy, nearly identical interior layouts.

Although the apartment's standard floor plan would have sufficed, John and Polly were concerned that the layout and materials would not reflect their personalities or their aesthetic sensibilities. For a couple whose lives have been devoted to learning and art, self-expression in their home mattered a

▓ Rolling barn doors of steel and sand-blasted glass replaced a solid wall in a retirement apartment unit. The doors allow the study to become part of the living room when the doors are open. When the doors are closed, the study serves as a guest room.

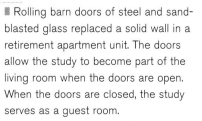

▓ The University Retirement Community is a village of 400 units housed in two apartment buildings. Each unit's facade is identical. The developer allowed one couple to alter the standard floor plan and then adapted some of those changes in other units.

great deal to them, and they wanted the apartment to feel more like an artist's loft than like a cookie-cutter retirement unit.

Luckily, the developers of the community—a board of former university academics—were happy to improve John and Polly's floor plan with the couple's design input. The couple hired Fu-Tung Cheng and Cathleen Quandt of Cheng Design, a Berkeley architectural and design firm, to help them assert their individual tastes and needs by customizing the floor plan and upgrading the materials package.

Flexing Fixed Space

The original plan for the apartment consisted of four rooms—a narrow, combined kitchen, a dining- and living-room area in the middle of the layout, flanked by a den/guest room on one side, and a master bedroom and master bath on the other—each separated by walls and by a rear hallway.

The House We Always Wanted

"WE KNEW WE DIDN'T WANT TO WAKE UP IN THE MORNING IN A SPACE THAT WASN'T BEAUTIFUL. WE HAVE TAUGHT, DRAWN, PAINTED, AND COLLECTED ART FOR MOST OF OUR LIVES, AND WE WANTED TO BRING OUR OWN BRAND OF AESTHETIC INTO OUR APARTMENT IN THE RETIREMENT COMMUNITY. "

—POLLY AND JOHN, HOMEOWNERS

■ Open or closed, the large glass doors let light—from the study windows as well as a kitchen skylight—penetrate the recesses of the apartment.

▌A few custom architectural tweaks turn a standard, boxy apartment into a custom-quality home. The ceiling for the dining-room and living-room areas, raised and angled around air ducts, delineates space between the kitchen and living areas while creating space to hang pendant lighting.

A MODEL BLUEPRINT

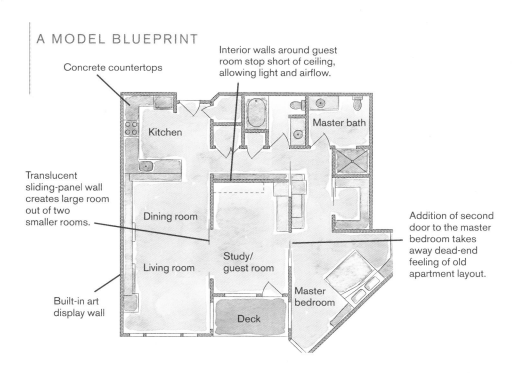

Concrete countertops

Interior walls around guest room stop short of ceiling, allowing light and airflow.

Kitchen

Master bath

Translucent sliding-panel wall creates large room out of two smaller rooms.

Dining room

Addition of second door to the master bedroom takes away dead-end feeling of old apartment layout.

Living room

Study/ guest room

Built-in art display wall

Master bedroom

Deck

The architect rearranged the floor plan so that the kitchen, dining, and living areas would take up the left side of the apartment, giving more room for the bedroom suites. The back hall from the original floor plan remains intact, but special materials have been added that brighten up the nearly hidden location.

Although the kitchen in the plan was somewhat open to the adjoining spaces, high upper cabinets made the room feel cramped and claustrophobic. The couple's number-one priority in the new floor plan was to redesign the kitchen.

Since Polly and John planned to have all but one dinner a week in the community dining room, the kitchen was designed to look like part of the living room and dining room as a way of creating a more sociable atmosphere. To connect the space to the living areas, cherry-veneer cabinets, which look more like built-in furniture than kitchen cabinetry, were installed partway up the corner wall. The exposed drywall above the cabinets helped make the space look more like the living areas as well. Storage drawers placed below the stainless-steel counters keep the space above the counter opened up and barrier free to the apartment's social areas.

▌ For added storage and display space, a 7-foot-long precast concrete sideboard runs below the plaster wall built for art displays, then ties into the cherry and stainless-steel kitchen counter. Cheng Design created the upright concrete slab on the right, and the stainless-steel oven hood in the background.

▌An angular slab of concrete establishes a focal point in the apartment. Set into the top is a fossil shell found in limestone. The concrete shape is also functional because shelves on the kitchen side provide valuable storage space in the small area.

▌ ARCHITECT'S NOTES

Concrete Ideas

"In limited spaces like this, precast and colored concrete helps to make a bold, expressive statement. It is a practical material—people can rest their arms on it—but it is also a piece of sculpture, a piece of poetry. Imbedding the fossil in the top is my way of echoing what we find in nature. It puts time in perspective. It took 125 million years to form the fossil and six hours to cast the concrete."

—Fu-Tung Cheng, Cheng Design

Considering the Details

More structural changes helped open up the original floor plan and make the space flexible. Rolling barnstyle doors made of sandblasted glass replaced a partially removed wall that separated the living and dining rooms from an enclosed den. When open, the doors now double the living- and dining-room space. When closed, the room reverts to a study and private guest room.

A flexible floor plan also meant something else to Polly and John. The couple needed adequate space to fit a number of pieces of furniture they acquired over the years. To make sure their furniture would fit into the redesigned floor plan, the couple took photos and exact measurements of each piece and gave the figures to the architect. The architect integrated the furniture specifications into the floor-plan drawings, with fractions of an inch to spare. The architect's challenge was to make sure the furniture was placed so that it would not block the flow of space.

▌A 10-inch-wide ammonite (a fossil shell) and flecks of stone imbedded in the concrete divider create a piece of art in the kitchen.

A bookcase runs the length of the back hallway, replacing a solid wall and transforming the bland space into a library. The floor-to-ceiling pocket door, inset with sandblasted glass, closes off the master-bedroom suite while letting in light from the apartment.

Accessibility with Style

The couple wanted to ensure that the floor plan would remain open and spacious to anticipate the couple's future needs. As a result, the apartment is designed throughout with 3-foot-wide doors and hallways, which meet the code set by the Americans with Disabilities Act (ADA). Each counter and vanity top in the apartment remains open underneath for wheelchair access. The architect reconfigured the bathroom by swapping the positions of the sink and toilet to create room for a limestone and slate roll-in shower, designed by Cheng.

Polly and John's adapted apartment layout and materials package combines a hip, youthful, contemporary aesthetic along with a pragmatic plan for the future. Rather than feeling small and closed in, the apartment seems open and roomy. The measure of its success is that the developer implemented the redesigned floor plan for 32 other similar units in their retirement complex.

The master bedroom has the clean, spare feel of an elegant, contemporary hotel room. Custom-made maple and cherry night tables, dressers, and cabinets fit perfectly around the bed. The bedroom's plaster walls are painted a cool gray to create a soothing sanctuary.

The long, stainless-steel grab bars are wide enough to double as towel racks. The design of the grab bars integrates well with the rest of the stainless-steel design elements found around the apartment.

AT HOME ON THE RANGE

Vanderpool, Texas

THOUGH IT MAY COME as a surprise after years of living harmoniously together in a family house, many couples don't always agree on where—or what—their dream home should be.

This Texas couple discovered this to be true after living for 20 years in a split-level house located on an acre of land. The husband loved the rambling floor plan of the house, where the couple raised three children. But following a long career as an ophthalmologist, he longed to live on a large piece of land and surround himself with acres of natural beauty that would bring him much deserved serenity. He found it 400 miles southwest of Austin's city limits, in a remote stretch of river valley nestled between canyons and limitless sky.

The wife, meanwhile, had started a late career in Austin as a risk-assessment manager. She loved city life and creature comforts, and she was content to stay in the family house. But she also wanted her husband to be happy. The solution was to build a weekend

▮ The floor plan respects the grade of the property, rather than altering the land to serve the design of the house. As a result, there are steps to access rooms throughout the house, such as the step down from the dining area to the living room. The 13-foot-high French doors are set on an 18-inch-high threshold—level with the surrounding windows—to capture as much of the skyline as possible by creating a window wall.

▮ Exposed rafters and pole supports are a nod to vernacular Texas buildings and help the modern ranch slip quietly into the landscape. Shed roofs tilt up to let in views of mountain ridges meeting the sky.

retreat, designed by architect Mell Lawrence. The new house, which is named Lazy-Eye Ranch, marries the couple's divergent life stages and tastes in a style Mell calls "rural modernism."

At 2,700 square feet, the ranch is smaller than the couple's family home in Austin, though the open flow of rooms and wide porches on all sides make it feel more spacious. And while the family house the couple still owns is private, light-filled, and comfortable, Lazy-Eye has modern conveniences and is really private—it's surrounded by 200 acres—with large windows to capture the views.

Centering the House on the Land

After reviewing the couple's file of photo clippings of preferred house styles, Mell understood that the one-level log houses they admired would be swallowed up in what the architect calls "the Bigness" of the southwest Texas country. So he created a house that both satisfies the couple's needs and connects to—rather than gets lost in—the land that the husband loves.

From the outside, Lazy-Eye looks like a cross between a contemporary hacienda and a sprawling series of utility barns. The abundance of porches is intentional: to dissolve the barrier between indoors and outdoors and to give even small, interior rooms a connection to the surrounding country-side. There are several open and screened-in spaces—some of them 14 feet wide, which is roomy enough for more than a couple of chairs.

Capturing Sounds and Views

The question of how to bring the enormous views of the valley, ridges, and sky into the house posed another design challenge. Gabled roofs, like those found on log cabins and farmhouses, would have limited views on two sides of the ranch house. Since the land was the reason the husband was drawn to this spot in the first place, a more site-specific house design was necessary to capture the sounds and views of this pastoral piece of property.

Peeled poles reinforce the interior's connection to the landscape. Here, in the earth-toned kitchen, the pole is the structural center of the house. The stone-topped cabinets divide the kitchen from the living room.

To accomplish this, Mell designed the house with huge shed roofs that tilt up to the canyon ridges to allow unobstructed views of the outdoors. The roofs, which are low at the courtyard level and high at the house's outer edges, are even less costly to build on a house than a design with peak roofs would have been. In addition, the tilted roofs create the space for large front walls and two-story-high banks of windows looking out on the scenery. The tilted shed roofs also cover wider areas of the porch than would have been possible if the house had a gable roof, allowing the homeowners to enjoy the outdoors on the protected porch, even during less than optimal weather. To keep the tilted roofs from blowing off due to the area's frequent strong winds, the galvanized metal covering is securely screwed onto the framing.

For the convenience and safety of homeowners and guests, a small foot light illuminates a rough stone step that leads from the kitchen into the living area.

■ Down a step from the casual kitchen, the bumped-out window wall creates a semiformal space for the dining room. Doors open, naturally, onto a porch.

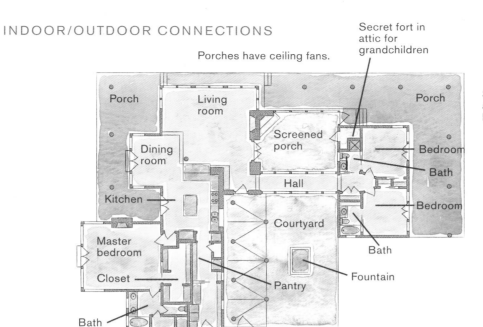

Porches have ceiling fans.

Secret fort in attic for grandchildren

Screened porch and hall separate hosts from guests.

Porch

Living room

Screened porch

Porch

Dining room

Bedroom

Bath

Kitchen

Hall

Bedroom

Master bedroom

Courtyard

Bath

Closet

Fountain

Bath

Pantry

Garage

Walls of Windows

The walls, which are adjacent to porches and to the views, lend themselves to the use of French doors. Every room has them, which allow prevailing breezes to run through the house, carrying with them the ambient music of crickets, birds, and local critters.

In the living room, custom cedar doors, measuring 13 feet high and 7 feet wide, were set on a high threshold so that they would be level with the adjacent windows and, when open, would function as picture windows themselves. When opened wide, the doors can be fastened to the window frames behind them so they don't blow in the wind. When all the doors and windows are open, the inhabitants enjoy the benefits of the country air within the social spaces.

Privacy Buffers

The master bedroom is located just off the kitchen not only for convenience but also for separation from the other social spaces and guest rooms in the house. The central living spaces—kitchen, pantry, living room, and dining room—are grouped together yet spin off one another for easy flow.

Another privacy passage is located off the living room. The screened porch provides a visual and acoustic buffer between the guest wing and the rest of the interior. The two guest rooms at the opposite end of the house are finished with native stone walls and timber floors. Though rustic in appearance, the comfortable spaces are replete with modern conveniences.

▮ Dappled light filters through the arbor of cedar posts and metal poles, sheltering the front entry from the sun. The protected entry-way, designed with rough-and-tumble stone walls and a slate floor, is a welcome contrast to the views of the expansive landscape.

■ Although it is large in scale and exposed to the outdoors, the master bedroom is still an intimate space because it is isolated at one end of the house and situated next to a protective grove of trees. The massive limestone fireplace gives the lofty room a strong focal point.

■ Lazy-Eye wraps around a small courtyard oasis on three sides, a design that centers the house in the vastness of the 200-acre property. The carport, left, is sided in gaped, weathered boards meant to let air circulate and to mimic the look of old barns.

The House He Always Wanted

"I HAD A VISION OF LIVING ON A MAJESTIC PIECE OF LAND—CRYSTAL-CLEAR WATER, MOUNTAINS, SECLUSION—BEFORE I EVEN FOUND THE PROPERTY. AND THEN, I WANTED A HOUSE THAT WOULD BE COMMENSURATE WITH THE SETTING, BLEND IN WITH NATIVE MATERIALS, AND BRING THE VIEWS OF THE VAST OUTDOORS INDOORS."

—HOMEOWNER

Choosing Native Materials

Baby boomers, such as this couple, have a regard for authenticity when it comes to the kind of materials used to build their homes. Local materials, such as slate, limestone, and aromatic cedar, help the interior and the exterior of the house blend in with the textured landscape of the countryside. Though the house is built with a minimalist palette of stone and wood, the materials are pleasing and soothing to the senses.

Along with the stone and wood, Mell found a way to incorporate metal into the structure. He found inspiration in the metal-roofed barns and utility sheds located around Vanderpool. The metal carport siding is spaced to duplicate the slatted light and shadows that fall through the old buildings Mell observed around town.

While the architect was drawing on regional architectural references, the husband decided to make himself at home and give names to different parts of the property from his own professional field of reference, such as Mount Myopia, Glaucoma Gulch, and Lake Amblyopia. The finishing touch was the husband's decision to name the property Lazy-Eye, a phrase adapted from the ophthalmologic term *amblyopia,* which means "lazy eye."

In the Company of Friends

Northern California

F OUR MARRIED COUPLES AND THREE SINGLE WOMEN in 1988, who then ranged in age from their mid 30s to late 50s, pooled their resources to build a sprawling, personalized community based on a deep desire to live among devoted friends during their retirement years. To find the ideal location on which to build their dream community, the group took summer vacations together before finally finding 19 acres of river valley and redwoods in northern California.

After interviewing six architects, they hired Fernau & Hartman, a firm that embraced the group's communal and ecological ideals. The design of the community, formally named Cheesecake, took shape over two and a half years, and the result is a U-shaped compound of four separate buildings totaling 6,000 square feet of interior space. (The property—once owned by an Italian family whose name translated to "cheese pie"—was renamed "Cheesecake" by the locals who used the land as a campground.) It includes a main lodge, bedroom wing, combination library and private apartment, and a workshop and storage space.

Designed by Committee

Cheesecake is an example of how design can represent the ideals and personalities of its inhabitants yet still be functional, flexible, and comfortable. For the compound to work, however, individual members had to participate equally in its design.

▨ The communal dining room opens into the living room of the main lodge, where a Rumsford fireplace is set in a concrete chimney and cast-concrete mantel. Though affordable and practical details define the interior, the spirit of friendship and community create a welcoming atmosphere.

▨ Most spaces in the compound have a double function, such as this combined stair landing and study in the main lodge. The stairs lead to second-floor bedrooms and a writing loft. Each member of the community has his or her own mail slot, shown at right.

■ Following the color coding on the architect's plans, common spaces at Cheesecake are placed in yellow buildings, while private rooms and apartments are located in red structures. The steep, covered stairway connects to the porch of the sleeping wing, to the right. Since the site lies in a floodplain, the four structures are perched on cement stilts.

■ Wine making (in the workshop building) isn't a group activity found in most retirement communities, but it works for this group. Cheesecake member Daniel Meyer's chardonnay won a blue ribbon at the county fair.

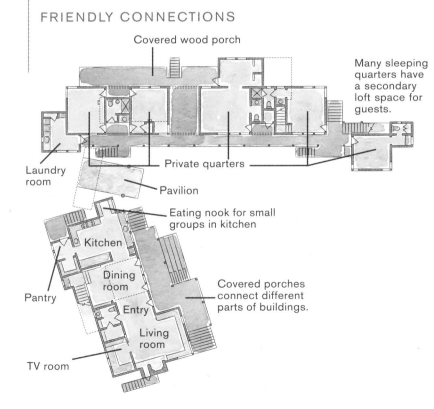

FRIENDLY CONNECTIONS

Covered wood porch

Many sleeping quarters have a secondary loft space for guests.

Laundry room

Private quarters

Pavilion

Eating nook for small groups in kitchen

Kitchen

Dining room

Pantry

Entry

Covered porches connect different parts of buildings.

Living room

TV room

FIRST FLOOR

Drawing on input from friends and from architect Laura Hartman, the design combines private and public rooms for both individual and group living. "We wanted the community planned so we couldn't just go off and be by ourselves," says Louise Browning, who with her husband, Dick, is one of the original couples who moved into Cheesecake when it was built. "The spaces are designed in such a way that you have to pass other people to get to the library or laundry. We didn't want anyone to become isolated. At the same time, there is so much open space that you can go the whole day without seeing anyone else."

Planned outdoor rooms—covered porches and walkways, trellised paths, tented platforms—added another 3,000 square feet to the complex, for a total of 9,000 square feet of indoor and outdoor space.

A breakfast nook in the communal kitchen adds extra counter space, allowing as many as eight people to prepare food or cook at one time. The decor is a mix of northern California Craftsman and salvaged industrial. Out the nook window, a trellis, which is a story and a half high, links the lodge to the private bedroom wing next door.

FACING THE FUTURE

The compound's master plan accommodates foreseeable lifestyle changes. Alterations to the compound require a vote by the entire community, and founding members agreed that changes must be designed and built by the original architects. So far, a handful of changes have taken place over the years. One couple added a sewing room, while another is contemplating the addition of a separate building for more space and privacy.

Other changes are inevitable. Doorways and halls, which are 34 inches wide, can already accommodate wheelchairs, but the architect also wisely left space in the floor plans for the addition of ramps and an elevator. The members built this sort of preparation into the design to smooth future transitions. Today, Cheesecake is a community of aging friends, facing the future with the same sense of self-reliance, freedom of choice, and love of one another that initially brought them together.

▌ A secondhand library ladder leads to the loft above a couple's apartment. Members pay for additional private spaces like this, but the community rooms are open to all.

Inexpensive and Recycled Materials

The materials used to design Cheesecake are basic, durable, and affordable for its members. The construction of the compound reflects more than budgetary considerations, however. It also expresses the group's simple and environmentally sensitive aesthetic. Wherever possible, recycled materials were used.

The buildings are sided with overlapping, horizontal cedar planks and plywood with vertical battens. The roofs are durable corrugated metal. The few trees that needed to be cleared were milled and used for decking and the dining-room table. Salvaged materials are used throughout the compound, such as the oak library ladders in the sleeping lofts, a kitchen island once used as a movie prop, and a patio of marble squares taken out of an old San Francisco hotel scheduled for demolition.

The buildings are color coded according to their use, just as they appeared in color on the architect's site and floor plans. Common areas are located in yellow buildings, and bedrooms and private spaces are tucked into red structures. The colors enliven the structures, emphasize their shapes, and express the group's vibrant spirit.

■ Louise Browning and her husband, Richard, live in this apartment in the 2,270-square-foot bedroom wing. With community approval and design input from the original architect, the couple was able to add a sewing room off the back of the apartment.

■ The main lodge is the center of the compound and houses most of the communal rooms. (The red dormer is a private writing loft.) The wide front porch with bleacherlike seating looks south into a quiet clearing in the redwood forest.

Four Connected Structures

The colorful shed-roofed buildings are clustered on the site and loosely connected by walkways and porches. The majority of common rooms, such as the cooking and eating areas, are housed in the 2,700-square-foot main lodge, along with a communal office and two upper-level apartments for members.

In the designing stages, members asked that there be only one kitchen and a dining room big enough for nightly communal dinners. Even though the kitchen measures just 260 square feet, the layout allows as many as eight people to work together at the same time. There's a cooktop, oven, food-prep counter, baking counter, a deep sink for cleaning vegetables, the stainless-steel island, a built-in breakfast table, and additional counter space in the adjoining pantry and mudroom. Members can eat breakfast and lunch wherever and whenever they choose, but they are expected to have dinner together.

The House Everyone Always Wanted

"WE WANT TO SIT ON OUR FRONT PORCH AND TAKE CARE OF EACH OTHER AS WE GROW OLDER. THAT BECAME OUR COMMUNITY'S CREDO. THE COMMUNAL DESIGN CAPTURES THIS FOUNDING SPIRIT, WHICH IS OUR LOVE FOR EACH OTHER AS FRIENDS."

—LOUISE BROWNING, CHEESECAKE RESIDENT

Next to the central lodge is the second structure: the long bedroom, or "dogtrot wing," as it's called among Cheesecake members. It houses five private apartments and a communal laundry room. Named for the roofed passages between buildings that are popular in the South, the front of the dogtrot wing has a veranda that leads to the third building on the property. The third building is a two-story communal library tower, which also includes a single, private bedroom for one of the members.

There's even more space for members on the site. A fourth structure is located 40 feet from the lodge and houses a game room, a 1,000-square-foot woodworking shop, storage space, and a small wine-making area—atypical activities for traditional retirement communities.

Equally important are the open spaces among the three linked buildings. Porches run across the front of the lodge and bedroom wing. Wisteria and climbing roses cover the wide, trellised paths in between. These open-air social rooms create the connective tissue that keeps members in touch with one another as they walk back and forth from activity to activity.

▌ Founded in 1988 by a group of former educators (who are still members), Cheesecake contains a second-story, 144-square-foot library, a space shared by the entire community.

Private Spaces

Private spaces are just as important as communal rooms to Cheesecake's participants. The compound contains eight bedrooms, plus overnight sleeping spaces in public areas for children, grandchildren, and friends. In addition, other rooms serve as semiprivate spaces, where members can steal away for a few minutes of solitary rest or with another member for personal time. In the main lodge, a small TV room in the rear of the building can be closed off from the more public kitchen, living room, and communal dining room.

Each member chooses what sort of private spaces they want to live in and be fiscally responsible for over a long period of time. One couple, for example, paid extra for a private bathroom, while the other members simply share bathrooms. To avoid squabbles over space, however, rooms were assigned to members by the architect when she designed the compound. Hartman approached the process in a democratic way, by assigning rooms based on each member's needs and wishes. It turned out to be the ideal way in which Cheesecake members could create their own special place within this sprawling community of lifelong friends.

A window seat in the library is a perfect spot for reading, napping, or accommodating overnight guests. Because the compound is set on 19 riparian acres, every room has a peaceful view of the forest, meadow, or water.

THE GEOMETRY OF TWO LIVES

San Francisco, California

T HERE'S A FREEDOM in modern architecture that exemplifies the empty-nester spirit. While drawing on earlier architects and influences, a modern house transcends the limitations of the past and can be shaped to fit around any sort of site, even when it's built just four blocks from the old family home. Though four blocks was familiar territory, it was far enough away for Otto and Idell Weiss to make a completely fresh start in a steel and glass house, perched on a steep hill, designed by architect Peter Pfau.

For 40 years, the couple raised three children in a typical 2,400-square-foot 1960s California home with four bedrooms. For nearly that long, Otto commuted to a downtown office, and once the children were gone, Idell turned a small bedroom into a sewing room/art studio and also commuted to a nearby artists' colony to paint.

The design idea behind the new house was to consolidate two lives and two daily routines—his and hers—for a couple who wanted to continue pursuing separate careers but do it together, under one roof, and without having to leave home. The architecture of the house highlights the geometry of these two joined lives. The modern, two-box composition gives shape to that idea and, in the process, expands the realm of possibilities for empty-nester living.

▋ Within the modern context of a sleek, open kitchen and family room, wood in many forms—maple floors, Douglas fir and maple ceilings, cherry cabinets, mahogany doors—ties the interior to the natural world. A breakfast area is in the foreground.

▋ A steep, wedge-shaped lot helped define the modern, fan-shaped architecture of the house. A wedge of steel, glass, and hardwood decking joins the two main boxes. All of the windows are commercial-grade storefront systems, able to withstand harsh coastal weather.

180-degree
views of the city

▊ Otto and Idell Weiss' modern empty-nester house, which is located four blocks from the old family home they once lived in, juts out from a hillside to take in views of San Francisco Bay and the city lights below.

The House
We Always Wanted

"WE WANTED A LARGER HOUSE BECAUSE WE COULD AFFORD IT AND BECAUSE WE WANTED OUR CHILDREN AND GRANDCHILDREN TO BE ABLE TO STAY HERE WITHOUT FEELING CRAMPED. WE WANTED A HOME OFFICE AND A STUDIO, AND THE LIVING AREA TO BE ON THE TOP FLOOR FOR THE VIEWS. MOST OF ALL, WE WANTED A MODERN HOUSE THAT WAS WARM AND INVITING."

—OTTO AND IDELL WEISS,
HOMEOWNERS

The Circumstances of Site

Long before making the decision to move, the Weisses would pass by an undeveloped, odd-shaped lot located a few hills behind their family house. Sloping south and wedge-shaped, the property's narrow edge faced a neighborhood cul-de-sac, but its wide, open side had commanding, 180-degree views of San Francisco and beyond, including the Bay, the Sunset district, Lake Merced, and the Pacific Ocean.

It's a challenge to design any kind of house on this sort of site. The couple wanted privacy on the street side but wanted the design of the structure to embrace all the views on the opposite side of the house.

An immediate problem, though, was gaining the support of adjacent homeowners, who for years had enjoyed unimpeded views across the empty lot. Peter was able to meet and talk with the neighbors, showing them illustrated diagrams of the proposed new house and listening to their ideas before getting the go-ahead to move the project forward as planned.

The result was a modern, wedge-shaped house to fit into the wedge-shaped building lot. To achieve this, the three-story house consists of two rectangular boxes, one slightly longer than the other, set at angles and connected by a central, trapezoidal wedge. The joined structures fan out down the site at an angle, capturing the best views for the couple while leaving neighborhood views intact.

A small sitting room at the upper edge of the house makes the master bedroom feel like the penthouse suite of a sophisticated metropolitan hotel. Large pocket doors close off the area at night. The door to the left leads to a deck for al fresco viewing.

Lots of space in the master bathroom and a low vanity and mirror make the room accessible while maintaining the kind of grace and style this empty-nester couple is used to enjoying in their home.

After 40 years of commuting, the husband decided to work from home. By positioning his office on its own floor in the public box of the house, with direct access from the entry hall and main staircase, clients can come and go without disrupting—or being disrupted by—home life.

Linking Three Levels

The lowest of the three levels of the house is tucked into the steep hillside and contains two guest bedrooms and a small kitchen for the children and grandchildren, plus an exercise room with sauna. The middle level, or first floor, is accessible by a small courtyard and entry and includes the garage and master suite in one of the boxes, the main staircase and home office in the other. The top, or second floor, contains the main living spaces, such as the living room in the smaller box, and the central kitchen, family room, and art studio in the larger box.

The central trapezoid—or wedge—does more than just hinge and link the two angled rectangles. It is a multifunctional space, providing an entry at the narrow end of the house, a widened art gallery on the first floor, and a formal dining room on the top floor. Broad decks fronting the space on both levels expand and heighten the spectacular views. The glass wedge appears to visually penetrate the boxes on either side, so that the three forms appear to be one house.

Blending Work with Home

The beauty of the floor plan is the way in which it allows the couple to have their private space and enjoy one another's company, too. The boxes are each designed for separate functions, which means that business and home life easily coexist in the new house.

Although Otto was in his 70s when the house was finished, he wasn't close to retiring from his lifelong career as an investment adviser and accountant. He was just ready to end the commute and the drudgery of trying to find a parking space downtown. By giving the first floor of the smaller box over to a home office, just off the entry and main stairs, clients can meet with him while enjoying the breathtaking views of downtown San Francisco, without intruding on any of the daily activities going on in the rest of the house.

It was after years of painting in a small, converted bedroom of the old house that Idell longed for a real studio with adequate light and an abundance of empty wall space to hang her work. Her new studio sits over the garage—a 400-square-foot room with soaring ceilings and large, blank walls. Though it lacks views of San Francisco and the Pacific Ocean, the space has something of greater value to an artist—a windowed wall of northern light.

▮ The glassed-in wedge is a multifunctional space, which connects the main boxes, circulates traffic, unifies views between the main boxes, and functions as a formal dining room with dramatic top-floor views.

THREE-WINGED PLAN

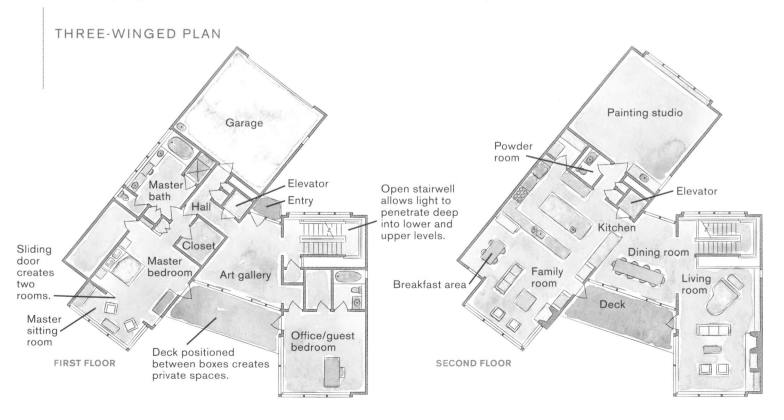

FIRST FLOOR

Garage

Master bath

Hall

Elevator

Entry

Open stairwell allows light to penetrate deep into lower and upper levels.

Closet

Master bedroom

Art gallery

Sliding door creates two rooms.

Master sitting room

Deck positioned between boxes creates private spaces.

Office/guest bedroom

SECOND FLOOR

Painting studio

Powder room

Elevator

Kitchen

Dining room

Breakfast area

Family room

Living room

Deck

From the upper deck that connects the living and family rooms, Otto and Idell enjoy the sweeping view of city lights, the San Francisco Bay, and the Pacific Ocean in the distance.

A steel staircase connects the three stories. The windows between the staircase and entry courtyard have a subtle tint to provide privacy and modulate the light.

PLANNED ACCESSIBILITY

Orthopedic surgery inspired Idell to request an elevator for the new house. The elevator's main mission lies in the future, when the owners might need to use it on a more frequent basis, not in the present. The couple wanted to make sure they built a house that they could stay in for the rest of their lives.

Located just inside the entry and the garage hallway, the elevator services all three levels of the larger rectangular box. The Weisses are active and make the effort to use the main stairs on the other side of the house as much as possible for exercise. But the elevator does get some use now and then because Idell finds it convenient to use when she is loaded down with groceries or with painting canvases.

A Modern Mix of Materials

Though the boxes are clearly in the modern style of architecture, the house is far from the cold and sterilized environment often equated with contemporary design. Peter made sure the house would be warm, inviting, as well as intellectually stimulating, through the mix of materials he used to design the home's exterior and the interior.

Each box has its own palette of exterior materials used to distinguish the public and the private areas of the house. The bedroom, kitchen, and studio wing, which is oriented to the east and to morning light, is sided with cedar. The western rectangle, containing the office and living room, is clad in smooth cement plaster. To articulate its difference from the two main boxes, the wedge is sided with a metal skin. The windows form a commercial-grade storefront system designed to withstand the ocean's brisk wind and rain.

These distinctive treatments carry over into the interior, where Peter mixed a multitude of woods that unite the two boxes and the deck—mahogany doors, maple floors and ceilings, exposed beams, and built-ins of clear-finished cherry—with steel, stainless-steel mesh.

The use of materials also affects the couple's workspaces. Idell's studio, with its high walls for hanging canvases and its large windows endowing the room with northern light, feels like an artist's loft. Her husband's office floor, reached by a modern staircase of steel and glass and outfitted with filing cabinets and couches, resembles the kind of sophisticated, professional commercial space he once commuted to on a daily basis. By design, the couple lives in a house filled with promise as two careers and one life move forward under the same roof.

Idell's studio, above the garage on the street side of the site, is the only room in the house without a view—but it's intentional. In place of views are big panels of clear, northern light, the best light for painting. The other walls are high and bare for hanging canvases to dry.

PART TWO

Just the Two of Us

The House as Retreat

TOGETHER ON THE RIVER

West Virginia

Lthough Tobey Pierce and Anne Winter built a house only 75 miles away from the three-story row house in Washington, D.C., in which they raised their four children, moving that short distance brought them a new lifestyle. Although their capital home had ample space, it was rare to find a private moment. Together, they dreamed of building a getaway in the country where, if only on weekends, they could be alone together.

By the time they found a seven-acre parcel high above the Potomac River, the semiretired couple had already developed an ideology of living in harmony with the land, the architecture, and one another. Working with architect Mark McInturff, they developed plans for a small but stately home located high above the river. The river house served the couple's ideals and wishes so completely that what was once planned as a weekend and vacation house evolved into a full-time retirement home.

The result is a 2,300-square-foot house with three sections divided into a central living space and two wings—or pavilions—accessible to each other by structures that the architect calls bridges. The sections not only create private, separate spaces but also break up the structure so that it does not appear as a large mass sitting heavy on the river bluff. The way the spaces relate to one another makes this relatively small house feel roomy without adding square footage.

▌The screened bridge between the main living spaces and the guest wing serves as the front entrance to the house. Unlike the shorter bridge to the media wing, this room is casual with exterior decking and an open, raftered ceiling.

▌Beyond the front steps of the house is a stone pier that doubles as a storage room beneath the farthest pavilion off of the screened bridge.

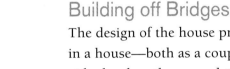
Suspended between piers, the screened entry bridge allows for water runoff and serves as a path between the front and the back of the house.

Building off Bridges

The design of the house presents the way Tobey and Anne envision living in a house—both as a couple when children and friends visit and as individuals when they spend time on their own. This sense of separation is important to Anne, who likes the flow of an open floor plan but wants acoustic privacy. The concept of private and separated spaces is also evident in the second-floor master bedroom—the only room on that level—where Anne practices yoga in seclusion.

Wide hallways connect the three sections of the house while also serving as narrow rooms. The shorter, enclosed bridge, which leads to the study, is formal and private; it contains a powder room and art collections from the couple's family and travels. The longer, screened-in bridge brings visitors into the guest room. The space also doubles as a summer porch and as a casual entry vestibule. Both bridges close off from the main section with double glass doors, satisfying Anne's need for acoustic and visual privacy from guests.

The guest bedroom is positioned at the one end of the house, far from the core living area. The antique apple-picking ladder, at right, climbs to a cozy sleeping loft for friends' children and future grandchildren.

▌A floor-to-ceiling window lets views penetrate from the kitchen into the media room through the short connecting bridge. A hallway urn, filled with ceremonial clubs and spears from West Africa and masks from Guatemala, tell of the homeowners' lifetime of travel and adventure.

■ Lowering the living room by three steps and raising the master bedroom on the floor above allow the ceiling to expand up to 12½ feet tall—a generous contrast to the cozier spaces with lower ceilings throughout the rest of the small house.

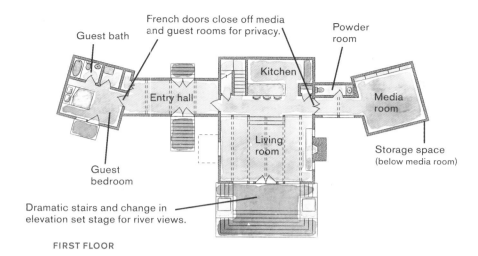

Guest bath

French doors close off media and guest rooms for privacy.

Powder room

Kitchen

Entry hall

Media room

Guest bedroom

Living room

Storage space (below media room)

Dramatic stairs and change in elevation set stage for river views.

FIRST FLOOR

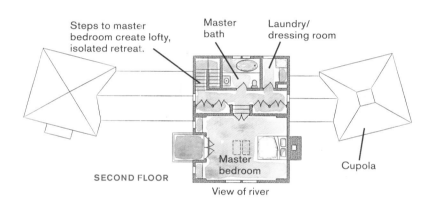

Steps to master bedroom create lofty, isolated retreat.

Master bath

Laundry/ dressing room

Master bedroom

Cupola

SECOND FLOOR

View of river

■ The front of the house is modest and faces a meadow with hints of river views. The bridges that connect the pavilions have a low profile from this side of the house.

Choreographing the Space

Mark refers to this evolution of spaces as "choreography." The way the couple wants to move around in the house and the way the house looks out over the river informs the design of the structure.

Although most kitchens become the heart of a house, they tend to be relegated to the rear of a home. Mark placed the kitchen front and center on the site to capture the best vistas and the views of the setting sun while Anne cooks and talks to family and friends. The location of the kitchen also provides Anne with a full view of each arriving guest. The view from the kitchen lines up with the large living room and French doors that lead to the two-story river-view porch, which is perched 6 feet away from the river's bluff, so that Tobey and Anne feel at one with the water.

Less Is More

Tobey and Anne's house is also a case study in the ecology of home design. "We felt an environmental responsibility that no space be wasted and that every square foot have a use," says Tobey. "We wanted the house to be the opposite of a McMansion."

The design of the staircase from the kitchen up to the master bedroom is just one example of the couple's pragmatic approach to living. The staircase is not walled off nor is the center of attention, but it is fully utilized with cubbyholes under the stairs for spice jars, cookbooks, and a collection of prized ceramics from the couple's travels. At the same time, the staircase possesses a strong but humble architectural presence. The landing and cubbies under-

■ Thin wood mullions, painted black, cause the windows to stand out as an architectural element close up but disappear against the view. From this vantage point in the house, the cook can see who's coming to dinner.

■ One of the ideas on the homeowners' wish list was that the kitchen
be located in the center of the house.
They also asked the architect to eliminate any upper cabinets in order to
install a large window with unobstructed views outside. The central
hallway doubles as a seating area at
the kitchen island, but it is separated
from the living room by a broad flight
of stairs. The slender posts frame
the rooms without interrupting the
flow of light.

neath the staircase anchor the two sets of stairs that angle upward in opposite
directions. The balusters are built with thicker stock than is typical to create
a robust design element.

Considering the Environment

The couple practices environmental responsibility inside and out. Pruning,
rather than felling, trees permits natural air-conditioning to course
throughout the house. The central area and pavilions sit on stone founda-
tions, but the bridges, suspended above the terrain with footpaths running
underneath them, allow water drainage.

Building with salvaged materials is another form of ecology used to
build the house. An antique orchard ladder ascends to the guest-room loft.
The rescued cypress doors come from old buildings in New Orleans. The
floors and the fireplace mantel were milled from old, dusty heart pine
beams taken from a warehouse in Massachusetts.

■ The private and spacious master bedroom
is located above the living room and up an
additional three steps from the second level.
In this energy-efficient house, skylights (not
shown) vent warm air in summer. The room
has clear views of the sunrise and the river.

Crossing the Bridge

"A relatively small house such as this one can be either a simple box that you move around in or separate parts that you move between. The spatial relationships between the parts make the house appear sculptural. The parts are rotated to follow the brow of the hill, and as you walk across each bridge, you become aware of the landscape. This design increases the connection to the land but also keeps intact the sense of separation."

—Mark McInturff, architect

■ Mount Vernon, 100 miles downstream from this home, inspired the building's design. Though the scale of the house soars on the bluff, the natural cedar siding and casual, exposed rafters help the structure blend in with the site without stealing thunder from the views.

■ In building the house, much of the river terrain was left in its natural, rocky state, making it an ideal site for a house just for the enjoyment of the local birds.

There is no wasted space, and every part of the house is used in some way throughout the year. The couple spends time on the screened and river porches from late spring to early fall, but the inside of the house is designed for the winter months. Although the walls and windows are well insulated and the three sections of the house have independent thermostats, in cold weather the owners can be found snuggled close to the wood-burning stove in the study or the energy-efficient Rumsford fireplace in the living room. "As the seasons change, we change the rooms we live in," Tobey says. The hearth is elevated and lengthened to serve as an additional, warm fireside seat.

The little house on the river proves that it's possible to live small, in harmony with nature and with one another, without having to give up human creature comforts or style. "We feel we're creating a model for empty nesters," Tobey says. "You can have a house that's space and energy efficient but also very beautiful."

▌ The house was designed around 8-foot-tall French doors and full sidelights. The doors lead from the living room to the two-story porch perched on a steep bluff overlooking the river. The framed mullions are thin and painted black so the windows won't overpower the views.

A Shipshape House for Two

Seattle, Washington

When Steve and Pam Zeasman told their architect what they wanted in a new house, they requested "something cool." The couple, who are partners in a construction company, have spent much of their lives raising their family in a 1915 cottage overlooking a bay. But, they also spent family time cruising around in a vintage mahogany sport fishing boat. So, it was only fitting for the couple when they bought one of the last undeveloped lots on Alki Beach in Seattle and began planning a home—with a focus on water—for just the two of them.

When it comes to home design, the couple's philosophy is decidedly nautical. Having worked together on other projects over the years, the architect Philip Christofides knew what the couple had in mind: A house should be compact, with every room possessing one or more purposes. The form of the house can be simple and preferably casual, but like fine boats, the materials, finishes, and details inside and out must be of the highest quality.

Careful planning went into their three-story, 2,700-square-foot house on the beach. Philip designed the Zeasmans' house to resemble a triple-decked ship that is permanently dry-docked and exposed to salt, air, wind, and moisture 365 days a year. The exterior had to be tough as well as low maintenance, since the couple work, travel, and spend a considerable amount of time on the water. But it's the design of the Zeasmans' house itself that maximizes the precious land it sits on.

■ Strict zoning codes often found on waterfront sites, such as this one on Seattle's Alki Beach, can result in efficient house designs. This narrow house packs a lot of space into three stories.

■ The inverted floor plan of this three-story house lifts the kitchen, living room, dining room, and deck high above the beach and the public park located next door. Even with 14-foot-high ceilings, the open plan of the top level feels warm and comfortable. Mahogany doors and trim, used throughout the house, reflect the owners' passion for boats.

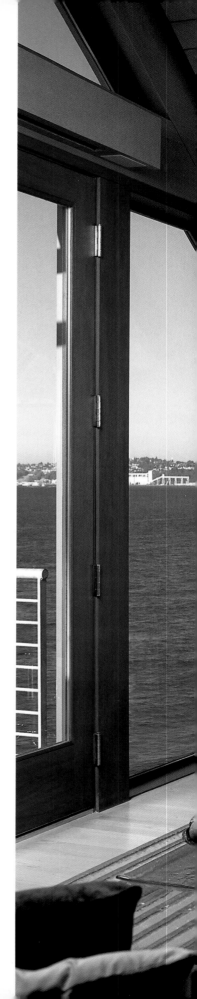

A COMPACT PLAN

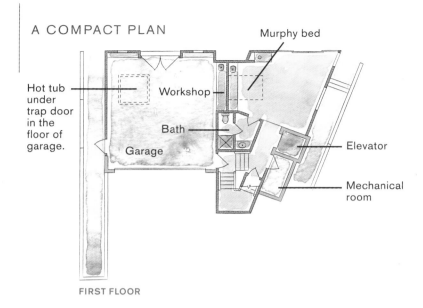

Hot tub under trap door in the floor of garage.

Murphy bed

Workshop

Bath

Garage

Elevator

Mechanical room

FIRST FLOOR

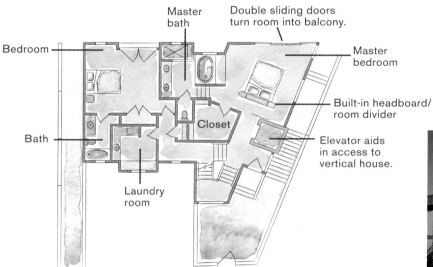

Master bath

Double sliding doors turn room into balcony.

Bedroom

Master bedroom

Built-in headboard/ room divider

Bath

Closet

Elevator aids in access to vertical house.

Laundry room

SECOND FLOOR

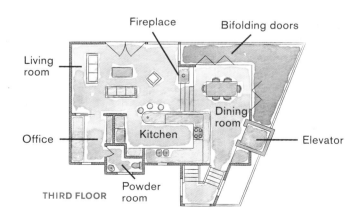

Fireplace

Bifolding doors

Living room

Office

Kitchen

Dining room

Elevator

Powder room

THIRD FLOOR

■ The narrow lot called for a two-part entrance alley distinguished by a stone floor leading up to the front door and a semiprivate concrete fence that creates a walkway down to the beach.

■ Squeezed between an apartment building and a busy park, the design of Steve and Pam Zeasman's three-story home gives the couple privacy, style, and unfettered views. The exterior—built with cast concrete, Brazilian cherry and metal siding, stainless-steel railings, and mahogany doors—demonstrates Steve's love of materials.

The main entrance opens into a glass-faced stair tower, which encloses vertical circulation in a corner of the house to conserve valuable square footage. The Dutch door design is deliberate—the top can be left open to let in air and light but prevents full visual access from passersby.

Designed around Zoning

The property, west of the city, is one of the last beachfront lots with no bulkhead, leaving it vulnerable to storms and erosion. The design of the house is driven by the stringent regulations affecting setbacks, footprints, and building heights.

The site lies just 20 feet from the high-tide mark, so to keep crashing surf from damaging the house, the lowest level of the house is built on a slab several feet above the sand. The slab's design is cantilevered and flared to repel waves. The garage side is raised an additional 30 inches above the other side of the house but for a different reason. Because the distance from the street to the house is so short, the driveway had to be at a steep angle. Raising the header of the garage by 30 inches, however, helped minimize the incline.

What's more, the busy community presses in on the Zeasmans' property from all sides. Alki, considered the Venice Beach of Seattle, is popular with bikers, skaters, and sunbathers. An apartment building and public park flank either side of the house, so privacy, light, and views were important issues in the design of this house.

■ The vaulted ceiling on the third floor helps to divide the open kitchen and living room. The 14-ft.-long peninsula serves as breakfast and lunch counter, with built-in china cabinets and wine racks for space efficiency, just like a well-planned boat would be crafted.

An Inverted Floor Plan

Given the highly public nature of the site, the three-story plan is inverted to give the Zeasmans privacy. The open kitchen and dining and living areas, usually located on the first floor, are hoisted to the top level, high above the eyes of the people on the street, park, and beach. The master bedroom, guest bedroom, and laundry room are located on the entry level, a few steps above the street. Tucked under the middle floor, just above the beach, is the two-bay garage—with a hidden hot tub—and a room that leads out to the beach. A set of exterior stairs can be retracted in stormy weather.

The 30-inch variance between the garage and the beach room affects the entire house, rippling through the rooms to create a perception of a split level on each of the floors above. The varying height solves the garage problem. It also creates a sense of drama on the upper floors by juxtaposing higher and lower spaces and angled views.

Multipurpose Rooms

This small house on its crowded site has more surprises. The compact floor plan forced rooms to take on multiple roles. For example, the beach room on the lowest level does extra duty as a family, TV, and guest room.

The creation of multipurpose rooms continues on the other side of the lower level where the garage is located. This space might very well be every man's fantasy garage. A hot tub is hidden under the spot where the car is parked, a bar is set up on top of the tool chest, and French doors lead directly out to the beach.

A small, concrete courtyard out front and the dining-room deck on the third level represent the house's only private outdoor spaces. The prowlike deck wraps this corner of the house, then angles sharply outward rather than

■ ARCHITECT'S NOTES

A Peaked Roof

Pushing the main spaces up to the highest level might have been a mistake had local building regulations not worked in the owners' favor. The city awards a 10-foot height bonus for beach houses with peaked rather than flat roofs. The bonus is meant to discourage the building of big boxes and to keep the waterfront looking more residential in nature. Here, the measure allowed for a 14½-foot vaulted ceiling in the dining room and a 12-foot ceiling in the elevated kitchen and living room. "All modern architects hate peaked roofs, but we'll take the space."

—Philip Christofides,
Arellano-Christofides Architects

The elimination of a corner post in the dining room leaves unobstructed views out to the water. A gable truss is cantilevered over the corner, supporting the roof and the folding glass doors. With the doors opened, the room appears to float off the house toward the outer deck and into the horizon.

Instead of logs, a living room fireplace of perforated steel heats refractory balls, which glow and cast heat.

Just like a boat berth, the second-floor master bedroom fits into tight quarters. To expand a sense of space and enhance views of the water, the master bath is left open to the bedroom and balcony doors. (A toilet, however, is tucked into a small closet out of view.) A built-in TV, to the right, and drawers in the headboard and under the bed are ways the architect consolidated storage space.

following the outlines of the house. The deck appears to be floating off into the horizon because there is no intrusion of support posts. Indoors, right off the deck, the panoramic views are uninterrupted, seen through several sets of bifolding doors. The view is one magical aspect of this home. The rich, high-quality materials used to build the exterior and interior of this retreat brings another layer of distinguishing design to this house on the beach.

Weathering the Site

Steve, a builder, is passionate about the craft of building a home and wanted nothing less than quality construction and materials. The exterior of the house is a hybrid of modern and traditional materials including concrete, metal siding, stainless-steel railings, and aluminum window systems, but also jatoba (Brazilian cherry), Honduran mahogany doors and frames, and clear, vertical cedar. The rear decks are waterproofed with fiberglass, a material that weathers well in the harsh wet climate.

The same mix of materials carries over into the interior where the predominant design elements are created out of wood. Not surprisingly, mahogany is the featured wood used throughout the house, as it is in the construction of classic boats that Steve admires and collects. The wood's rich, deep colors warm up the rooms and set a tone—casual and sporting yet polished and elegant—that runs throughout each room. Touches of mahogany are found everywhere, from the rear garage doors to the front door, and from kitchen cabinets to guest-room built-ins. The house is clearly a boater's paradise on land.

From the siting of the house to the materials used to construct this nautically inspired home, the Zeasmans' beachside sanctuary embodies the passion of two people who are continuing a long and great voyage together.

The entry stairs and elevator (its beige door visible in the background) are located right outside the master bedroom, but the sliding-glass bedroom door is frosted for privacy. The custom-made headboard is 18 inches deep—wide enough for file-cabinet storage drawers, retractable night tables, and substantially sized storage cubbies.

The headboard in the master bedroom adds another layer of privacy, even when the sliding bedroom door is open. The center niche of the headboard also frames a view of the bay seen in the distance from the bedroom window. Out in the hallway, the elevator is hidden behind a standard residential wood door that matches doors in the rest of the house.

Federal regulations prohibit building a bulkhead on this property, which is the last unprotected lot on Alki Beach. Set 20 feet away from the high-tide mark, the beach house rests on a cantilevered slab with a lip that curls up to repel surf. Roll-up doors in the foundation hide storage space below the garage for kayaks and boat gear.

A beach-level suite, with full bath and a private entrance off the beach, gives guests their independence. Handsome built-ins—television screen, fireplace, minibar, hideaway bed—allow for multiple uses: as a TV room, guest room, post-beach party room, and grandchildren's play area. And it is far away from the master bedroom and the entertainment areas located on other levels.

The House We Always Wanted

"ONCE THE KIDS WERE GONE, THE HOUSE BECAME OUR FOCUS. WE WANTED A STYLE THAT EMBRACED OUR LIFESTYLE, WHICH IS CASUAL AND ENTERTAINING, BUT WAS RICH IN MATERIALS AND DETAIL WITHOUT BEING STUFFY. IT WAS IMPORTANT THAT WE HAVE A SPECIAL SPOT FOR US, AS WELL AS SEPARATE SPOTS FOR THE GRANDKIDS AND FOR OUR ADULT GUESTS."

—STEVE ZEASMAN, HOMEOWNER/BUILDER

The Zeasmans have the ultimate West Coast garage. When the Porsche backs out of the bay, block-and-tackle rigging hoists the stainless cover to the hot tub, which is sunk into the garage floor. (The cover, shown at left, is secured to the wall.) Rear glass and mahogany doors open directly onto the beach.

A Couple's Island Lodge

San Juan Island, Washington State

IT'S POSSIBLE, as many empty nesters are discovering, to have a home that is both public and private, has large and small spaces, and is designed to meet a couple's needs while still remaining family oriented. All of which Donald and Kathleen Peek wanted in their retirement lodge, which was designed by architect Geoff Prentiss. The lodge, located on a steep, wooded lot, is the place where the couple spends their summer months, frequently joined on weekends by their children, grandchildren, and friends.

Of the house's many accomplishments—the seamless integration of the structure to the site, the high degree of craftsmanship inside and out, and the practical use of space—the house succeeds best in its ability to accommodate a large, extended family while allowing Donald and Kathleen to feel comfortable when they're home alone.

A Fusion of Styles

Although an indigenous, Shingle-style architecture exists on the island, the Peek's house incorporates several mainland influences that the couple likes very much. One is the Craftsman style, notable for its use of wood and woodworking skills. The other—and more significant—is the traditional Adirondack Camp style, which the couple has admired for so long.

▍ The full-length porch and deck act as a plinth or base, balancing the house on the sloping land, while bleacherlike steps serve as a family gathering spot. Ten-inch-wide posts and a chimney of local fieldstone tie the house to the wooded, rocky site. In the distance lies Orcas Island and, beyond, the Pacific Ocean.

▍ Cozy seating areas, all with views to the lush greenery outside, create small retreats for homeowners and guests to go to for quiet time within the large living spaces of this house.

A covered walkway leads from the high road and down through the woods to the main entrance of the house. The entry arcade also introduces the formal axis, or central line of the house's design—here, a series of formal spaces—that runs through the house. Peeled fir posts, exposed rafters, and rough-cut cedar shingles signal a woodsy, handcrafted interior.

The House They Always Wanted

DONALD HAS LONG ADMIRED THE GREAT CAMPS OF UPSTATE NEW YORK, WHICH MATCH STRUCTURE TO LANDSCAPE AND FEATURE NATIVE MATERIALS, A RUSTIC LOOK, AND CENTRAL GREAT ROOMS. HE AND KATHLEEN WANTED ALL OF THIS, WITH A DEGREE OF QUIET AND PRIVACY FOR TIMES WHEN GUESTS VISIT.

By breaking up the large structure into three parts, the house achieves a scale that pays homage both to traditional island cabins and to larger Adirondack camps.

When the couple has the house to themselves, they can close off the great room and master bedroom suite from the entry hall and guest wing by shutting pocket doors of ribbed glass.

In the Peek's house, all of these elements find seamless expression in a poetic vision of the camp style. But the design and construction also serve the more tangible, present-day needs of the owners. The result might be labeled "refined rustic," or perhaps "elegant camp," style. Whatever the label, the house fits right into the rocky, forested, brooding side of the island, but it does so with grace and with 21st-century comforts.

Seasoned Materials

The use of wood in the camp echoes the refined-rustic theme. The wood also highlights the baby boomers' longing for authenticity and the use of

In the great room, a 25-foot-long ridge sky-light bathes the otherwise shaded space in daylong sunlight. By surrounding the large space with alcoves and with openings into adjoining rooms, the room is integrated and animated with daily life rather than isolated. A small game room occupies the alcove on the left. The doorway at the end of the living room leads to the office, which, in turn, leads to Donald and Kathleen's private master-bedroom wing.

quality materials in the house. Having owned a family timber company, the Peeks knew what quality of lumber to select. The house is covered in sea-soned cedar shakes with rough, uneven edges, culled from a local sawmill, to replicate the look of early-20th-century cabins and camps. The siding was made to look further aged by adding a coat of iron sulfate. Then local finish carpenters, many of whom have boatbuilding skills, tightly sheathed the house against winter storms. Peeler-poles—the posts supporting the entry and back porches—were harvested on the site and stripped of their bark before installation.

The rugged exterior of shakes and poles makes a transition to smooth, polished paneling and trim in the interior of the house. Most of the

CLUSTERS AND EDGE ROOMS

Spaces for retreats, also known as clusters or edge rooms, work well to divide up large areas of a house. Homes for one or two that double as family-gathering places need these types of retreats for privacy and quiet-time getaways. Donald and Kathleen built three retreats within their house. Without needing to post signs on the doors, the way the spaces are designed gives the impression that they are private domains.

One retreat, just off the great room, is the couple's office built just big enough for two people. Up four steps from the great room, the long entry hall leads to the library, and at the opposite end of the hall is a bunk room for grandchildren and young guests. The rooms are 60 feet apart—and the library walls have been soundproofed—for a reason: One space is intended for reading and reflection, the other for rambunctious activity.

▮ The small library is a pleasing contrast to the great room and the sweeping porch.

▮ Donald and Kathleen's small home office is outfitted with a wraparound desk and shelving to hold a computer, copier, and fax machine. Though the room is wired with multistrand communications cable, Western red cedar paneling and a peaked ceiling create a warm, rustic atmosphere.

■ Where common household functions might be hidden away, this utility hall, located behind the kitchen, is not only practical but also creates opportunities for social interaction. Kathleen's desk and storage cabinets line the left wall. The concrete floor, with radiant heat, is patterned after a children's hopscotch court.

■ The warm and inviting kitchen is made even more spacious by its accessible location. It opens up to the utility hallway off the entryway, the great room, and the guest wing for easy access.

GETAWAY SPACES

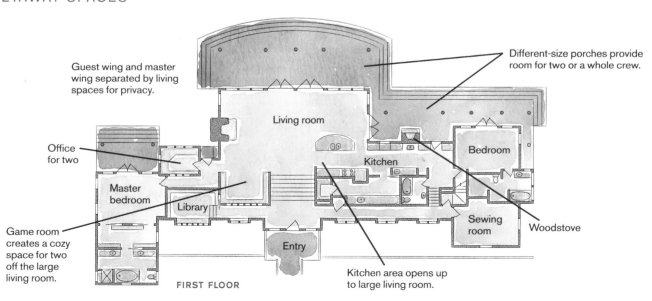

Guest wing and master wing separated by living spaces for privacy.

Different-size porches provide room for two or a whole crew.

Office for two

Living room

Bedroom

Kitchen

Master bedroom

Library

Sewing room

Woodstove

Game room creates a cozy space for two off the large living room.

Entry

Kitchen area opens up to large living room.

FIRST FLOOR

paneling, flooring, and ceiling strips on the inside were sawn from a very old, 8-foot-diameter hemlock log, which most likely drifted down from the Olympic Peninsula and was salvaged from the ocean.

Materials found elsewhere in the house owe more to function and convenience than to aesthetics. The industrial-strength, corrugated-steel roof is durable and low maintenance. The floor in the utility room and pantry are radiant-heated concrete. And three rooms are wired with Category 5, multistrand cable for communications and high-speed Internet access—not the typical wiring found in most camps, lodges, or retirement homes.

Lighting the Interior

The land and the house sit on the thickly forested east end of the island. In winter, the house gets early light but by late morning, it is cast in a chilly shade. What's more, the main architectural styles the owners favored—Craftsman and Adirondack Camp—feature deep roof overhangs and porches that further blocked the available light.

▍Outdoor rooms, like this cozy sitting area around the porch fireplace, carve out private areas independent of larger spaces. Readily accessible from the pantry, kitchen, and great room, the porch also handles an overflow of guests during family gatherings.

The challenge was to bring light into the house in imaginative and aesthetically pleasing ways. Skylights with painted aluminum frames straddle the roof ridges in three places. In the great room, the skylight runs the length of the 25-foot-long ceiling, pouring in thick bars of sunlight onto the walls and wood floor for much of the day. Shorter ridge skylights brighten the entry hallway and master bath.

As if to draw all of the available sunlight from the site, double-hung windows installed in the interior wall of the entry hallway spread the light deep into the house—especially into the office and the game room. In the summer, windows are open so a current of ocean air from the outer windows softly breezes through the house.

Creating an Intimate Camp

At 4,100 square feet, the retirement camp might seem large for some couples. But by breaking up the plan into clusters of rooms and by creating and scaling the biggest room to intimate proportions, the house is the just the right size for the couple, plus all the visiting family and friends.

Balancing out the public and private spaces are cluster rooms, which allow the house to expand when the couple has guests, then contract when it's just the two of them at home. More important for the owners, the clustering of space allows the master-bedroom suite and main living areas to be sealed off from much of the house. From late fall to early spring, Donald and Kathleen close the door to the guest wing and the pocket doors at the bottom of the entry-hall stairs to create a cozy one-bedroom suite that is roughly half the size of the whole house.

■ The master bath, located off the owners' bedroom, has a more refined and serene sensibility than the other, more casual bathrooms in the house. Cased in Douglas fir, the soaking tub sits on a limestone slab and looks out to a secluded, mossy bank on the northwest corner of the property.

■ The master-bedroom suite is situated at the opposite end of the house from the guest rooms and the grandchildren's bunk room, yet it is within a few steps of the home office and the great room. In addition to the bedroom, the suite contains a spacious master bath and a private porch overlooking the water.

A separate but spacious deck off of the master bedroom is a key design element reserved for the enjoyment of empty-nester homeowners. The Peeks have up-close water views from their private bedroom deck.

Sensitivity to how the house is used at different times also applies to the central gathering place. Down a short flight of steps from the entrance, the house opens into the 24-foot by 40-foot great room, surrounded by a cluster of rooms rather than by walls. Furniture helps divide the big space, but it's the use of proportion and scale—high wainscoting and tall windows and doors—that gives the room a smaller, narrower feel and makes it comfortable whether twelve people or two inhabit the space.

In addition, edge rooms—the smaller, semiopen spaces off the great room, such as the game-room alcove and mudroom—function as independent spaces. Though the rooms tie into the larger room, they are far enough apart and sufficiently set back to serve as small getaway spaces when the house is full of guests.

REFINING THE RANCH

Brentwood, California

Agrave;FTER 25 YEARS OF RAISING three children in a two-story, 5,000-square-foot house filled to the brim with the stuff that families tend to accumulate, Suzi and Steve Gilbert were ready to simplify their lives. The couple bought an older, 2,300-square-foot ranch-style house on a corner lot in suburban California, happy to find a reasonably priced home close to friends and family. Then they asked architect Buzz Yudell to turn the house into a casual, relaxing, European-style villa.

Rather than leveling the house, which is the fate of many ranch-style homes from the 1950s, Buzz remodeled it, maintaining the home's single story for easy mobility. The design of the house is sophisticated in its materials and detailing, but the layout keeps the Gilberts' children and grandchildren in mind. Buzz added space over the garage for a study and storage area, and he lengthened a bedroom by 7 feet, creating a 700-square-foot addition, giving guests and visiting grandchildren more room in which to sleep.

■ The original living room was small and dark, but removing doors and walls and adding a cathedral ceiling transforms and enlivens the space. Doubling the thickness of the existing walls gives them more of a substantial presence. The wide baseboard unifies rooms that are located on two different levels.

■ The new, double L-shaped floor plan of the house creates a number of courtyards around the property. Stairs lead up to a second-story study, which is far removed from the rest of the house. Below, the angled exterior doorway leads to a long, narrow hallway that runs along the bedroom wing.

Low-Maintenance Exterior

The Gilberts wanted to spend their time relaxing, not on maintaining the house. To reduce upkeep, the architect clad the house in simple materials, including a durable, standing-seam zinc roof, which replaced asphalt shingles, and stucco applied over the old shingle siding. Since the stucco is integrally pigmented (meaning the color was mixed into the mortar), it will never need to be repainted.

What gives the exterior its elegant appearance is the restrained application of the stucco, which was steel troweled for a smooth finish. As the stucco weathers, it will vary in tone and become darker and richer, adding depth to the walls.

A Collage of Courtyards

Walls of softly colored stucco form courtyards around the house—an important way to expand the living space of the house. The courtyards were the couple's idea. Suzi wanted space so she could devote herself to gardening, and they both wanted privacy to enjoy

▌The design of this walled yard makes the space inviting. The walls are high enough in places to define the private courtyards yet low enough elsewhere so they won't block neighbors' views or isolate the homeowners. The Douglas fir gate to the front entry courtyard and light-colored earthy tone of the stucco walls are more welcoming than inhibiting. A zinc band on the top and bottom of the gate adds a contemporary yet casual detail. Low-maintenance, crushed granite replaced the patchy lawn of the original landscape.

A COURTYARD PLAN

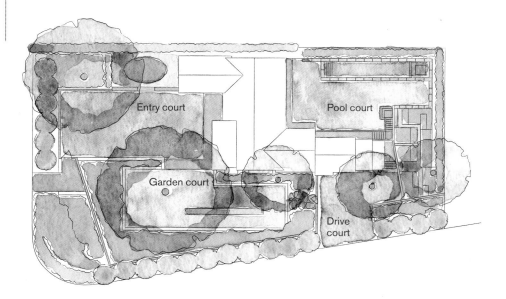

Entry court

Pool court

Garden court

Drive court

OLD EAST ELEVATION

NEW EAST ELEVATION

▊ A wide doorway and spacious entry replaced the old, narrow door and cramped dark corridor in the house's original floor plan.

▊ The house sits on a corner lot, exposed to the street on two sides. Adding a low wall and granite ground covering creates a private and dramatic entry court with the feel of a casual European villa. The steps and lower walls help settle the building into the various levels of the landscape, define the different outdoor rooms, and offer cool, courtside seats for relaxation.

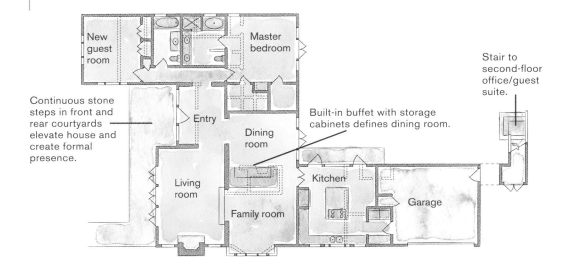

Continuous stone steps in front and rear courtyards elevate house and create formal presence.

New guest room

Master bedroom

Entry

Dining room

Living room

Kitchen

Family room

Garage

Built-in buffet with storage cabinets defines dining room.

Stair to second-floor office/guest suite.

▌ ARCHITECT'S NOTES

Exterior Rooms

"This project was all about creating an inviting and well-lived-in home, one that feels full and warm when there's either just two people in it or a party of 100. It was also important to the owners that we make the most of the relationship between the exterior rooms and the landscape. The exterior spaces help expand the boundaries of what is a modestly styled house, but the rooms can be occupied in and of themselves, with a form and character all their own."

—Buzz Yudell, Moore Ruble Yudell
Architects & Planners

▌ The architect enclosed the corner lot with corridors of lawn and narrow flower beds to define the boundaries of the house from the street. Low steps mark living areas while making it easy to move about when transitioning from the master bedroom into the pool courtyard.

▌A pair of French doors in the 210-square-foot master bedroom opens onto the lap-pool courtyard behind the house. On the opposite side of the house from the entry courtyard, it is a private space, shielded from the neighbors by gardens.

the serene outdoor setting. Since the house is set back far enough from the street and from neighbors, it was possible to create four distinct courtyards as transition spaces that connect the interior to the landscape.

The entry courtyard, in front of the house, is the most public of the outdoor spaces, serving both as the main entrance court and as an overflow entertainment area off the living room. Stone steps on two sides of the courtyard help define its boundaries and separate it from front and side gardens. Since the area gets a lot of traffic, it was given a surface of decomposed granite (a hand-packed, dry soil), which is durable but is softer than concrete and needs little maintenance.

Behind the house, a rear courtyard is composed of lawn, cutting gardens, and a lap pool. An abundance of flower beds fill the narrow

▌The hallway off the front entry once led into a closet. Now, it leads to the bedroom addition. The hall is a gallery for family photos.

courtyards on either side of the house. The entry courtyard, in particular, feels European—like an outdoor cafe in perpetual summer, simultaneously refined and casual. This old-world feeling continues inside the house.

The Flow of Interior Space

Inside the front door, the vestibule is grand because of its generous proportions and uncluttered space, but it is crafted with informal materials, such as natural maple flooring. The entry introduces guests to the open, airy feeling found throughout the house.

The original floor plan of the house was composed of small, isolated rooms. As a result, circulation patterns throughout the house were restrictive, narrow doorways limited access, and small windows in each room made the spaces claustrophobic. The architect removed several walls and closets, as well as one fireplace, to open up the interior. The widened doors create vistas to other rooms and offer greater accessibility. The result is an easy, open flow between the kitchen, living room, family room, and dining room.

It didn't take extensive rebuilding to create the personal oasis of the homeowners' dreams. The Gilberts were able to achieve their sanctuary by simply rearranging the interior space of an older home and opening it up to the outdoors.

▌ Floor-to-ceiling corner windows bring an abundance of light into the formerly cramped, dark ranch-style living room.

▌ The rear kitchen window wall has unobstructed views of the pool courtyard. Green and black granite countertops are easy to keep clean and stand out against the natural maple cabinets. Bar stools around the island create a third eating area and make this as much a room for entertaining as it is for cooking.

▌ The dining room looks out into the entry courtyard. A serving cabinet for additional storage replaced the original fireplace. The dark green honed granite cabinet counter complements the warm Douglas fir trim. During large parties, the doors are flung open and tables are set up in the courtyard for the overflow of guests.

Reached by an exterior staircase that looks like a piece of sculpture, the new study added over the garage doubles as a retreat with an extra guest room, private bath, and exercise area. Built-in file drawers and bookcases keep papers hidden away. The 240-square-foot study could easily convert to an apartment for a live-in aide if the need arises.

A breakfast table overlooks the rear garden and pool. The idyllic setting is also an ideal spot from which to monitor grandchildren's activities.

Windows with horizontal panes echo the lines of the traditional ranch-style house. The abundance of windows in the house visually connects the interior to the property's numerous outdoor rooms.

Field of Dreams

Northeastern Indiana

John and Cynthia Ruhaak raised two children in a 3,000-square-foot town house in the Chicago suburb of Lincoln Park, Illinois. When the children were grown, the couple moved to a smaller apartment in the city. The house they dreamed and talked about, however, was something quite different. The couple loves farms, open space, and unpretentious buildings of simplicity and grace. For eight years, they searched, mostly out West, for a remote piece of property on which to build a retirement house. They finally bought a 10-acre parcel of former farmland in Indiana. The setting of the couple's field of dreams affected the design of the house.

Architect Dan Wheeler, known for his Shaker style–inspired architecture, conceived the house as three separate structures. These he designed in farmhouse vernacular but with a cosmopolitan touch influenced by the late architect and sculptor Donald Judd, an advocate of minimalist, barrack-style design. The enclosed courtyard differentiates the main, two-story house from the utilitarian buildings on either side.

▌Facing page: By siting it on a crest between rolling meadows and a sheltering forest belt, architect Dan Wheeler enabled the house to take command of the land. In its simple yet sophisticated design, the house stands in stark relief against the prairie sky. Below: Inside, the simple farmhouse turns more formal.

A Balancing Act

Two opposing design concepts balance the appearance of the house. The house is a sophisticated farmhouse, with both new and familiar forms. While the structure has the simplicity of Shaker buildings, there's also a complexity to its organization that makes it a forward-looking design.

There's also a balance experienced at the entrance to the main wing of the house. Approached across a graveled, outer courtyard, visitors encounter a unique facade, one that breaks traditional rules but in a welcoming way. The entrance is a recessed doorway set in the southern end of the wing. However,

The House They Always Wanted

Untamed land drew John and Cynthia to Indiana, and the site informed the design of their home. They wanted the landscape to be experienced in different ways in different parts of the house. They also wanted a courtyard as a controlled, hidden space that would contrast with the open meadows surrounding the house.

a replicated doorway across the bumped-out bay of windows poses the immediate question: Which door leads to the way in? Upon closer inspection, it's apparent that one "door" has no stoop or doorknob, revealing that this is no door at all. It's just a window, and it is part of the design for balance and for fun. The composition gives the facade a pleasing symmetry, without revealing too much of what's behind it.

Exposed to the Wildlife

Meanwhile, the rear and the northeast corner of the main wing demonstrate an open, uninhibited side to the otherwise modest house. Topography and siting make this possible. Behind the house, large blocks of mullioned glass frame the primary views—the Indiana dunes and, on clear days, Lake Michigan, farther to the north—from the living room on the first floor and from the master bedroom and bath. Even the bathtub is fully exposed to the environment. Since this is a house designed with just the two of them in mind, however, and since the only creatures crossing the property are coyotes and wild turkeys, who minds?

The tension and balance between openness and privacy continues inside. There are no formal hallways in this house. Spaces open directly into other spaces—the front vestibule into the library, living room, and dining room; the dining room into the kitchen; and the kitchen and dining room into the courtyard.

First encountered to the left of the main entrance, the inner courtyard is a mystery with visual clues. The fence panels are held away from the posts with reveals to impart fleeting peeks of greenery.

Cleft-faced steps of Indiana limestone are in keeping with the practicality and graceful simplicity of the buildings. Though unadorned, the classic form creates a powerful looking formal entry.

The similar style of the bay window (left) and the door-style window (right) in this room give the house a symmetrical appearance from the outside. The built-in desk in the library floats across the bay window.

DESTINATION ROOMS

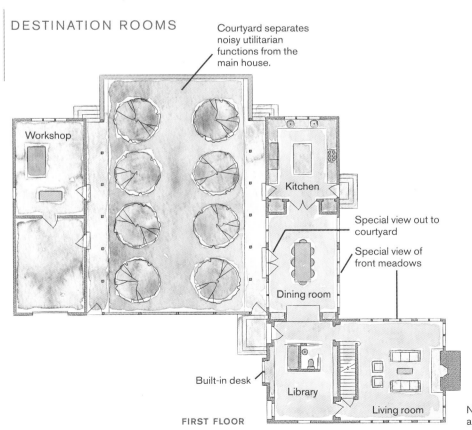

Courtyard separates noisy utilitarian functions from the main house.

Workshop

Kitchen

Special view out to courtyard

Special view of front meadows

Dining room

Built-in desk

Library

Living room

FIRST FLOOR

Once inside the front door, a light-filled hallway leads into the library or dining room.

Narrow rooms allow light and views from both sides.

■ Floor-to-ceiling windows in the living room help create drama—an indoor/outdoor room that embraces every aspect of the property including the prairie, the forest, and the sky.

■ A table in the living room captures all of the views to the southeast. The window composition turned what is basically a barn form into a contemporary structure of space and light.

Each Room a Destination

The relatively small home—just less than 2,600 square feet—has a layout that permits a couple to inhabit the same spaces without getting in one another's way. What's more, the architect expanded the perception of space by giving each room its exclusive vista, creating the space as a destination.

The library and second-floor guest room, which look out onto the front meadow, is one such destination. The master bedroom and bath, with sweeping views of the countryside, is another. The kitchen and dining room look out into the courtyard. The courtyard itself, grassed and lined with a gallery of crab apple trees, is its own, separate world.

In addition, if the dining room or kitchen becomes crowded, French doors from both rooms lead to the inner courtyard. John and Cynthia also have their own solitary workspaces: his is attached to the garage, where he works with wood, and hers is in the basement, where she weaves.

■ In the open yet cozy country kitchen, the center island was designed as a freestanding piece of furniture, which has found practical use as a breakfast table and gathering place.

■ Like many of the rooms in this house, the dining room is a flexible space. French doors and wide doorways help the room naturally flow into the courtyard, the kitchen, and the living room, while it remains visually separate from all three spaces.

On a clear day, the homeowners can see Lake Michigan from their master bedroom. The bottom transom is fixed, but casement windows swing out for uninterrupted views.

For a city couple who longed for wild, rural spaces, the master bathroom's orientation to the Indiana farmland provides both privacy—by virtue of so much distance between neighbors—and uninhibited views.

Pragmatic Shaker Style

The Shaker ideal of form following function, in simple but graceful ways, and it informed the design of the house from the start. Examples of this are evident in the choice of materials used everywhere in the house—materials chosen for their looks as well as for their relatively low cost and minimal maintenance.

The kitchen and dining-room floors are hand-troweled, radiant-heated concrete, which is easy to clean. The chimney stack is an exposed, galvanized flue, which is made of heated metal coated with nickel and zinc to prevent it from rusting. Aside from costing far less than a conventional brick or stone chimney, this stack looks right at home against the galvanized, standing-seam iron roof. ("Standing-seam" refers to the way metal sheets are folded and joined with a metal cap.) This type of roofing pays tribute to the old style of agricultural buildings, but it also has proven itself to be extremely weather worthy, lasting two to three times longer than asphalt roof shingles.

For the front steps and courtyard arcade, cleft-faced Indiana limestone was the material of choice because it was readily available and inexpensive. The cedar clapboard and tongue-and-groove siding was prestained a neutral gray to blend into the landscape.

Placement on the Prairie

Part of the art of this design is how it is placed within the landscape. The house's archetypal shapes command the landscape from the outside, and inside, the rooms are designed to take advantage of the site. The rooms use the space outside the windows to increase their relative size, scale, and character. While the larger rooms expand to encompass the prairie vistas and dunes, the other rooms let the trees serve as backdrops to create a more intimate scale.

By virtue of its simplicity and straightforwardness, this 21st-century house appears no more obtrusive on the horizon than a comely, 19th-century barn.

▌ In the rear elevation of the main wing, a second bump-out, deeper and wider than in the front of the house, encloses the living-room chimney, while giving the entire structure a sense of equilibrium. It overlooks a separate, courtyardlike garden.

PART THREE

Separate but Together

The House as Family Compound

AN OLD COTTAGE MADE NEW

Jamestown, Rhode Island

To MANY PEOPLE, the term "having the house to ourselves" equates with having lots of space. The principles of good design apply equally in homes of 1,000 square feet or 10,000 square feet, as this small gem of a vacation/retirement cottage, renovated by architect James Estes, illustrates. The house is also a classic example of how a couple can live their lives independently while sharing their time and space with visiting children and grandchildren.

Built in the 1920s, the 900-square-foot cottage was originally divided into a warren of small, dark rooms with low ceilings. After a Connecticut couple bought the place and began sharing it with family and friends, the more its space limitations became apparent. Adding a bedroom and bath off the rear of the house gave the couple a room to themselves but that didn't alleviate the cottage's cramped social areas.

So the owners turned to James, whose work they admired. The last thing they wanted was a beach house like others in the area that had been expanded out of proportion. The architect agreed to take the job on condition that the project would respect the scale and style of the original structure. He proposed a three-part renovation program to expand the social spaces in the main section and bring in light, add a freestanding guest wing for the couple's two grown sons and future grandchildren, and upgrade materials without sacrificing the character of the cottage or exceeding the couple's budget.

▉ Breaking through a low ceiling and tearing down walls turned an old, cramped and dark fisherman's cottage into a sunny vacation and retirement home for a couple who love the sea. The view at left is from the living room, looking into a sitting area and a corner of the kitchen. At right, the humble scale of the main house and addition is intentional, allowing the design to fit in with the neighboring cottages.

If the homeowners added a second floor for more room, it would have changed the low massing and the cottage's style and scale. Instead, a guest wing adds needed room.

The House We Always Wanted

"WE WANTED TO KEEP THE UNFUSSY, COZY FEELING OF THE ORIGINAL COTTAGE, WHICH WAS LIKE A CAMP FOR ADULTS. WE [NOT ONLY] WANTED PRIVACY [BUT ALSO] A SENSE OF THE OUTDOORS AND OF THE NEIGHBORHOOD. WE LOVE OUR NEXT-DOOR NEIGHBORS AND THE FACT THAT THEY CAN LOOK INSIDE TO SEE IF WE'RE AWAKE."

—HOMEOWNERS

The original closed, airless entry porch is now a covered walkway designed in a casual, rustic way, befitting the old New England seaside neighborhood. The walkway's red cedar posts, fir rafters, painted pine sheathing, and industrial light fixtures create a welcoming facade.

A Respectful Renovation

At the heart of this subtle renovation is a respect for the original building and its context. Both the house and the addition belong in the neighborhood of other casual, shingled cottages and Victorian homes a block from Narragansett Bay, an early New England coastal village. Both the house and addition fit in with the other casual shingled cottages and Victorians in the area. But by opening up the cottage interior—from floor to ridge, and from one end to the other—the parents' place seems twice its original size and feels brand new. All of this was completed without altering the exterior of the house or the surrounding streetscape.

Reclaiming Lost Space

James vetoed the addition of a second floor to the house because it would have changed the cottage's style and scale. To add space, he eliminated interior walls and ceilings, converting several rooms into a single area. The design creates a sense of vaulted space, which is visually and psychologically important in small houses such as this.

With the ceiling opened up, the exposed ridge beam gives the space a high, clean, airy look. At the same time, however, pulling down the walls and ceilings removed the structural supports of the gabled roof. Rather than

The dining room floats in the open floor plan and under the high ceiling. Square windows in the eaves, centered on the roof's ridgeline, bring in morning light.

reclutter the interior with collar ties or trusses or spend money on an unsupported beam, a slender post was tucked between two other vertical elements—the fireplace and the refrigerator.

A Piece of Sculpture

It's hard to believe that the handsome brick chimney, which is tapered and corbeled (or bracketed), was once encased within the walls and ceiling. In opening up the space surrounding the fireplace, it now stands as a piece of sculpture, in addition to functioning as a natural divider of the newly reclaimed space.

Since the fireplace adjoins the kitchen, the intervening space is the optimal place for a refrigerator. Befitting a 1920s cottage, the contemporary unit is encased in a high cabinet of vertical, 1-inch-thick by 4-inch-wide tongue-and-groove pine boards. The cabinet extends another foot at waist level to form a shelf between the refrigerator and the fireplace, which carries through to the opposite side of the fireplace, where it connects with a wide bookcase in the living room.

This island of brick and wood, fire and ice, form and function, divides the open space into the living-room, kitchen, and dining-room areas, without walls, doors, or ceilings. Far from being hidden, it is the focal point of the renovated house.

▎Added to the back of the parents' wing, the 180-square-foot master bedroom in the main cottage opens onto a private deck and garden.

Bringing the Outdoors Indoors

In addition to a choppy interior floor plan, the rooms were once walled off from views of the street and from the sounds and view of the water a block away. To open up the indoors to the outside, double sets of large, four-over-one windows replaced smaller units.

French doors are an easy way to break through solid walls and let in light and views of the landscape. In the living room, these doors lead to a side deck and a garden between the cottage and the guest addition.

■ Envisioned as a piece of freestanding sculpture, the fireplace and arched refrigerator cabinet also divide the entry, dining room, sitting area, and living room.

■ Vertical tongue-and-groove paneling in the kitchen is also used elsewhere throughout the house to tie the rooms together in early 20th century cottage style.

ORIGINAL COTTAGE

Old storage shed removed, and ocean views and eastern light regained.

Shed

Deck

Master bedroom

Dining room

Kitchen

Living room

Bedroom

Enclosed porch

REDESIGNED AND EXPANDED COTTAGE

Bedroom

SECOND FLOOR

Shed

Deck

Master bedroom

Kitchen

Dining room

Living room

Entry

Deck

Bedroom

FIRST FLOOR

Covered walkway serves as front porch and privacy screen from front to rear yards.

Two doorways greet guests entering the addition. One door opens into the ground-floor bedroom, a second to the stairs and the second-floor bedroom.

Built in the 1920s and renovated in the late 1990s, the original, one-story house, at left, was joined by a covered walkway to a new, two-story guest wing, which was designed for visiting grown children and grandchildren. The linearity of the walkway helps to balance the new and remodeled structures.

A Unifying Walkway

The key to making this arrangement work is in the two-story guest wing, which is separate from the main part of the cottage but is connected by a walkway. The original porch running across the front of the single-story cottage was once sealed off from the outdoors and was stuffy and seldom used. The plan called to replace it with a covered but airy walkway that continues past the main cottage another 20 feet to the guest wing. The walkway is symbolic of the relationships that take place here: parents and grown children, original house and offspring addition, and renovation and neighborhood.

The walkway's exposed rafters, rustic brackets, and industrial outdoor lanterns are the right look for a New England seaside neighborhood.

Because it is open, the walkway also connects the house to the back garden between the two buildings, framing and defining it as an exterior room and allowing anyone sitting out on the addition's rear deck to see who's coming to visit.

The Family Connection

A strong "family resemblance" exists between the cottage and the guest addition. Both are simple, shingled buildings, with similar-style doors, windows, and decks.

At the walkway's far end, guests are presented with three doorways with three entry options into the guest wing. The guest wing is designed with privacy in mind. One door opens into a sitting room, another opens into a set of stairs to the second-floor bedroom, and the third—a pocket door—is used to separate the space into two bedroom suites.

Like the cottage, both rooms are clean, uncomplicated spaces. This was accomplished by tucking the bathroom and closet on each level into a "saddlebag"—a two-story addition to the addition—rather than carving out space in the main guest rooms. The design and materials used in both guest bedrooms visually refer back to the main house.

The guest wing intentionally lacks a kitchen—and for good reason: Guests still have to gather together in the main cottage at mealtime, with no excuses for delays along the way.

To highlight the saddlebag, the architect made the bump-out look different from the rest of the house by cladding it in pale blue painted vertical boards rather than siding it in natural cedar shingles.

A SADDLEBAG OF SPACE

James prefers rooms to have clean lines that are uninterrupted by closets, bathrooms, or even shelving. To keep the new guest wing simple, he designed a "saddlebag" of ancillary, utilitarian space for storage and baths. The saddlebag is an architectural term coined by the architect, writer, and teacher Charles Moore, who needed to find a way to create a simple room with an unencumbered central space. In his words, he draped spaces around the core, "like so many saddlebags."

The saddlebag on this house is 4 feet wide and deep and two stories high on the far end of the guest wing. Rather than hide its existence, the extension is highlighted with vertical boards, a contrast with the natural shingles that cover the rest of the wing. As an additional touch, the saddlebag is painted a pale blue and the windows are trimmed in aqua.

Living outside the Box

A series of side and rear decks extend the living areas, as do the sections of yard they inscribe. The shed, once attached to the back edge of the house and separated several years before the renovation, is now located 6 feet away from the back of the house to help screen the kitchen deck and backyard from the neighbors. Moving the shed also cleared the way to a view of the bay from the deck.

Out in front, the porch walkway swings left to join a narrow deck off the living room. Steps down from the deck lead to an intimate garden between the cottage and guest house, and across the grass is yet another deck off the back of the addition.

All of these exterior areas are important to a couple that loves gardening and smelling the surrounding salt air. But the spaces also serve as additional places to simply relax, whether together with guests or apart—which most couples need to be from time to time.

One of the bedrooms in the freestanding guest cottage comfortably houses the couple's grown sons, but it's also designed with future grandchildren in mind. Double beds and low ceilings will make children feel right at home.

A rear deck off the kitchen is a private refuge from guests. The shed on the right was once attached to the house, but now it is located 6 feet off the back of the building where it helps screen the deck and backyard from neighbors while opening up the view down to the bay.

Visiting children need privacy, too, so the guest wing has its own backyard and deck. Ten feet separate the guest wing from the main house; sundecks and a small garden buffer the buildings.

A NEST FOR THE FUTURE

Seaside, Florida

IN THE 1980s, architect Robert Orr bought an empty lot in Seaside, Florida, just as prices began to escalate. He knew he would have to come up with an ingenious way to make the vacation and future retirement home he planned to build pay for itself over a long period of time, until he started using it himself.

Robert was drawn to Seaside's cozy, charming atmosphere, with its narrow streets that invite long, leisurely walks; small lots; and houses with front porches meant to encourage a sense of community. Soon after he bought the property, Robert's circle of friends in the young town grew when he married Carol, the landscape architect he had hired to landscape the grounds. Together, they continued to design a floor plan for their vacation home that is flexible so that parts of the house function in unison while other parts work independently.

A Tailored House

Because of the flexible floor plan, the 2,250-square-foot house can be rented out in whole, in sections, or as individual rooms to help cover costs. Robert also designed the house to be spacious enough so that he, Carol, and their extended family could have the house to themselves without stepping on one another's toes.

As a result, the house is composed of two separate buildings with a wise mix of public and private spaces. The design was also determined by the tight, 50-foot-wide by 100-foot-deep lot, which encourages structures with long, narrow buildings and rear porches. A series of footpaths that run

■ Rising 50 feet above the tropical vegetation and neighboring houses, and separate from the main wing of the house, the third-floor bedroom tower has its own staircase, private entrance, and porch. The tower wing has a casual, Western, roadhouse style that highlights its independence from the main family wing. It is a special, magical place that is easy to rent out when the owners aren't staying there.

■ This bedroom porch faces the front of the street and is high enough to look out over the neighboring metal rooftops and out to the sandy beaches of the Gulf of Mexico. A wide overhang prevents the scorching sun from overheating the room.

A house that accommodates both family members and paying guests needs at least one great room—like this combination kitchen, dining room, and living room in the main wing—where people gather before wandering off to their rooms or private porches. Despite a certain formality in the gleaming columns and cabinets, the room maintains a cool casualness with concrete floors, a bamboo ceiling, and ceiling fans.

Front porches off every bedroom nearly double the size of the 2,250-square-foot house. The proportions of the porches are intentional. If they were any wider, they would overshadow the interior rooms. If they were any narrower, there wouldn't be room for small groups of chairs, and it would have eliminated the passageway leading through to the rest of the house.

through Seaside and converge at the corner of the property inspired the 50-foot-high water tank–like tower, which serves as a landmark for walkers but also elevates the owners' views above neighboring houses.

The Main House

The home's two sections—a main house and a separate bedroom tower—are connected by two long, double-decker wooden porches. The two-story main house features a traditional floor plan that includes two bedrooms for either children or adult guests built over the first-floor master bedroom and great room.

Family and guests often convene in the great room, which is a combination kitchen, dining room, and living room. It is a place where people gather before wandering off to bedrooms or private porches in the main house or in the tower across the lower deck.

A Bedroom Tower

Across from the main house, the guest bedroom tower soars three stories to feature uninterrupted views to the ocean and into town. As in the main structure, a master bedroom occupies the first floor. A kitchen, small living room, and a sleeping loft for children are located on the second floor. The kitchen is located on the second floor for elevated views over the roofs of

The view of Seaside, Florida, is clear from the third-floor tower bedroom. As a young architect in 1982, Robert Orr helped design the traditional town, developing many of the ideas he would later incorporate into his own home.

SHARING A PRIVATE PLAN

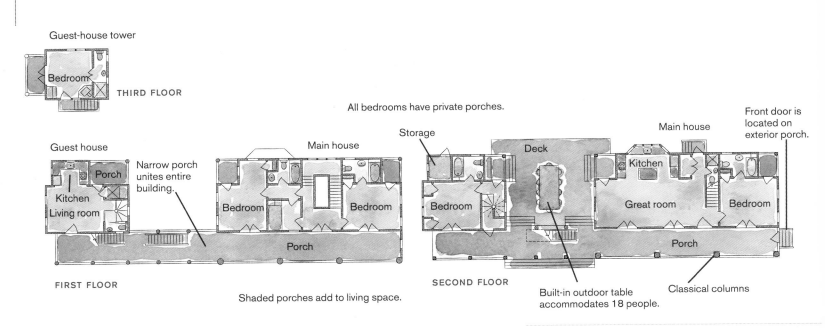

Guest-house tower

Bedroom

THIRD FLOOR

All bedrooms have private porches.

Guest house

Porch

Kitchen

Living room

Narrow porch unites entire building.

Main house

Bedroom

Bedroom

Storage

Deck

Bedroom

Main house

Kitchen

Great room

Bedroom

Front door is located on exterior porch.

Porch

Porch

FIRST FLOOR

Shaded porches add to living space.

SECOND FLOOR

Built-in outdoor table accommodates 18 people.

Classical columns

In the tower wing, a second, smaller kitchen opens into a living room and dining area, creating a separate living experience. The space is located on the second floor to provide privacy from the common deck and to elevate its views above the neighboring houses. The ladder leads up to a private sleeping loft.

All six bedrooms have private baths and private porches for smaller, more intimate gatherings. Bedroom walls are painted in warm, tropically inspired colors.

NOOKS AND CRANNIES FOR KIDS

Even before Robert had children, he conceived of the perfect vacation/retirement home with sleeping quarters for children. "I imagined a space that would stimulate fantasy and embed fond memories in the children for years to come," Robert says.

That once-imagined space is now a reality found in each part of the house. A bedroom on the second floor of the main house is designed with bunks that are stacked and tucked against a wall to look like a ship's berth. The bunks are partially enclosed by paneled archways so that climbing up into them seems more like the neighboring houses. A guest bedroom occupies the top floor, designed with privacy in mind so that it can be rented out at the same time the Orr family visits the main house.

time for an adventure than time for bed. In the tower section, a second-floor sleeping loft is similarly partitioned but perched high above the stairwell and accessed only by a tall, sliding ladder.

The little getaways are small worlds free from grown-ups, yet they are found within the walls of an active, extended family house. Getaways for children give adults more time to relax alone, and they are a pleasing contrast to the larger public spaces, such as the great room, dining deck, and colonnaded porches, which bring everyone together for fun.

The tower guest loft is partially concealed. Old-fashioned woodwork, reading sconces, and built-in cubbies for books and stuffed animals add to its cozy atmosphere. The durable, deep-sea blue walls are achieved with four to five coats of white and purple paint, rubbed off between layers, then finished with blue enamel and clear varnish.

Designed for Privacy

Each bedroom in the tower has its own small porch, which faces away from the main house. The bedrooms also have a separate entrance and locking exterior doors for the comfort of guests. The doors leading into the house are soundproof to isolate the bedrooms for a sound night's sleep. The third-floor bedroom in the tower has its own exterior staircase up to a private entrance and a side porch overlooking a lush garden of tropical vegetation.

Connecting Porches

Both parts of the house are connected by a second floor's back porch and by the dining deck. Robert designed the bedrooms in the main house and in the tower to face out to the street so that each one could have a small, private porch. He saved the large, full-length porch, which spans the back of the main house and the tower, for family gatherings so that they would be more private.

▍In a twist on the old notion of Florida retirement living, this contemporary Georgian-style house is composed of two independent wings connected by a common deck (the steps lead up to the third-floor tower bedroom). The arched and oval-shaped trellis shields the deck from the house next door. The outdoor dining-room table accommodates all 18 members of the owners' extended family in a private but spacious layout.

The long, two-tiered porches on the back of the house connect the independent bedrooms to this more communal space. The porches face east to capture morning light but also shelter guests from the hot afternoon sun.

The porches add about 1,800 square feet to the floor plan, nearly doubling the size of the house. Each bedroom feels larger and roomier with this borrowed outdoor space, which is accessible through French doors. Since the porches run the length of the main house and tower, they eliminate the need for interior halls, creating a roomier interior.

Together on the Deck

A lower-level deck also connects the main house and the bedroom tower. It serves as a family-gathering area that accommodates a 5-foot-wide by 12-foot-long dinner table, which seats 18 people. Most indoor dining rooms cannot fit a large seating arrangement like that, which also often requires the use of table extensions, card tables, or extra folding chairs. But the no-fuss outdoor dining area makes it quick and easy for diners to quickly come together and to take advantage of the fair Florida weather.

Renting the house makes sense for Robert and Carol, who are still involved in their careers. The final phase of the evolution of this house will be when the Orrs retire. They envision a few changes to the house. A bedroom in the tower will one day convert into a home office. Until then, however, the Orrs enjoy the privacy of their home when they please, even when vacationing guests are occupying some of the other parts of the house.

■ ARCHITECT'S NOTES

A Practical Design

"I had to design the house in a practical way, so I focused on the rental market and that influenced its design. I made the house very functional for big families that visit or rent in the summer by adding bunk beds for the kids. But the bedrooms function for couples who rent in the winter with private entrances and baths for each of the bedrooms. Many of our renters are empty nesters, and this is an ideal empty-nester house."

—Robert Orr, Robert Orr & Associates, and homeowner

■ Inspired by the Georgian-style homes of Charleston, South Carolina, the long porches on the house are supported by Doric columns. French doors from the bedrooms access the upper porches, offering a private escape from the evening gathering spot located on the ground-floor porch.

AN ADDITION FOR TWO OR MORE

Jackson Hole, Wyoming

WHEN DAVID AND LISA vacationed in the Grand Tetons years ago when their two children were young, little did they know the ski and resort town would become their future home. Once grown, both children left the family home in the Midwest to live in Wyoming. The parents soon followed. This sort of role reversal is becoming common among baby boomers, and David and Lisa were on the upswing of the trend in purchasing land near their kids.

The 1,800-square-foot house that came with the property dates to a mid-1980s development, built before the town's popularity boomed and land prices soared. Instead of razing the original structure, however, the couple and architect Stephen Dynia remodeled it into a guest house. They then built an adjoining wing—or pavilion—which had an open floor plan and was enclosed by an abundance of glass. The two-part project has turned the property into a retreat for the family and a private retirement lodge for David and Lisa.

A Tricky Site

Strict local zoning proved a challenge when the couple began designing and siting their dream pavilion. Since zoning originally mandated that

▍The massive timbers, native stone, and rusted steel gate of this empty-nester couple's house recall the early frontier buildings found in the region.

▍Wood, metal, and Montana moss stone combine to frame a private inglenook within the open 3,000-square-foot pavilion. A small window lets natural light into the otherwise dark and cozy space.

The original tract house (right) is connected to the new pavilion by an enclosed bridge. Rather than try to blend architectural styles, the pavilion's design minimizes the presence of the earlier structure, which now serves as a guest house.

the existing house be built 300 yards from a highway, the addition naturally had to stick close to the site.

To create visual and acoustical privacy on the highway side of the pavilion, the architect designed a V-shaped wall of raw steel over concrete blocks. To reduce more of the din from the road, earth was bull-dozed against the wall to form a noise-absorbing berm. The wall also leveled the sloping meadow for an out-door dining patio off the kitchen.

Meanwhile, a natural feature helped link the two structures. A creek bed is located between them, fed by the Snake River at high water and at other times by two artificial ponds, which were built to maintain a continuous water element. The idea inspired the 20-foot bridge between the pavilion and guest house, which gives everyone in the house privacy once the guests leave the pavilion and retire for the night in the guest house.

The new entry accesses both the outdoors and the bridge to the guest house. When the empty-nester owners want to be alone, they close and latch the door.

A 20-foot-long bridge straddles a creek and elegantly connects—and separates—the guest house from the couple's pavilion. Since the house sits within an earthquake zone as well as an area of heavy snowfall, metal cross-bracing is used to reinforce the structure.

The House They Always Wanted

AFTER RAISING A FAMILY IN A 1920S TUDOR HOUSE, THEN IN AN 1830S FARMHOUSE—BOTH WITH LOTS OF SMALL, CONFINING ROOMS—THE COUPLE CRAVED A CONTEMPORARY STRUCTURE WITH LARGE EXPANSES OF GLASS TO LET IN VIEWS AND LIGHT. THEY ALSO WANTED A FLOOR PLAN THAT INCLUDED ONE LARGE PAVILION, TO ACCOMMODATE SIZABLE GATHERINGS, AND A KITCHEN WITHOUT WALLS SO THAT LISA WOULD NEVER HAVE TO COOK IN ISOLATION.

A PLAN THAT ADDS SPACE AND PRIVACY

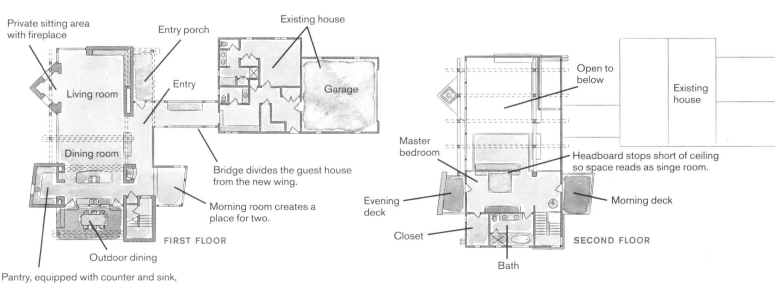

Private sitting area with fireplace

Entry porch

Existing house

Living room

Entry

Garage

Dining room

Bridge divides the guest house from the new wing.

Morning room creates a place for two.

FIRST FLOOR

Outdoor dining

Pantry, equipped with counter and sink, is semi-enclosed to conceal activities.

Open to below

Existing house

Master bedroom

Headboard stops short of ceiling so space reads as singe room.

Evening deck

Morning deck

Closet

SECOND FLOOR

Bath

The oversize interior furnishings in the kitchen match the mass and scale of the stone walls of the house. The large island, made of wood with a granite countertop, offers plenty of places for guests to sit and chat while Lisa cooks.

Though the massive stone wall marks off a hallway leading to the bridge, it allows the floor plan to remain uninterrupted and light-filled.

A Rugged Design

The 3,000-square-foot pavilion was designed as a long, open-ended rectangle with a 32-foot-high ceiling to match the towering Grand Tetons on the near horizon and to give the owners a feeling of wide-open spaces. Since David and Lisa are the only people who stay in this part of the family retreat, there are no walls or doors in the pavilion.

The choices of interior and exterior materials—from the walls of Montana moss stone and the rough-sawn timber trusses connected by black metal plates to the rusted steel walls—help this pavilion blend in even more with the rugged textures of the surrounding landscape. This combination of materials produces a house that looks contemporary, industrial, and rustic, all at the same time.

Stephen wanted to continue to blur the boundaries between inside and outside and used the design of the house as a tool to accomplish that. One way was to use large expanses of glass to help reveal the interior and exterior structures of the house. At one glance, the stone walls that support the trusses are clear and apparent.

The bedroom loft in the pavilion is suspended from a series of trusses and rods. The support system allows the loft to be open and airy, and it gives the downstairs long vistas around the stone masses.

David and Lisa's home office is nestled at one end of the loft, behind double-paned glass, and is tucked up under the roof so that it feels far removed from the rest of the pavilion.

The sitting area in the loft bedroom is just large enough for a small fireplace, where the couple can sit and look out at the snow-capped mountains. The high headboard (left) is a divider between the master bedroom and the home office, which is located on the other side of the loft space.

Intimate Spaces

The structure of the house may be revealed on the outside, but inside there's a sense of privacy. Smaller spaces branch off the pavilion to give the house a sense of scale and intimacy in comparison to the large and undivided main room. A morning sundeck off the kitchen and an evening deck off the master bedroom loft are outdoor retreats.

Inside, stone wall partitions penetrate the house in the kitchen and in the fireplace inglenook, causing natural separations within the open plan.

The rear door leads to a private patio with grill, dining area, and dramatic views.

At one end of the room, stone trusses enclose the fireplace in a triangular alcove. The dropped 8-foot-high ceiling, a raised hearth, and space for just a couple of chairs creates another private spot to view the Teton Range. These small but important interior spaces help visually ground the house by providing a needed sense of human scale alongside the revered mountains.

A Rustic, Rusted Finish

"The raw metal sheathing on the patio wall, as well as on the loft trim, bridge siding, and chimney exterior, was treated with myrrhic acid, then left alone to rust. The finish is evocative of old metal barns found in the countryside of the Wild West. Rusted metal works here in the West because it looks weathered, like stone or wood, and everyone out here likes the result. Since there's no acid in the air, the material never needs maintenance."

—Stephen Dynia, Stephen Dynia Architects

▌ On the western edge of the pavilion, a low, prow-shaped wall of earth and rusted steel is wedged into the terrain, forming an outdoor dining patio off the kitchen that wraps around the house on three sides. The wall shields the house, visually and audibly, from a nearby highway without blocking distant views of the Teton Range.

A SHIELDED SITE

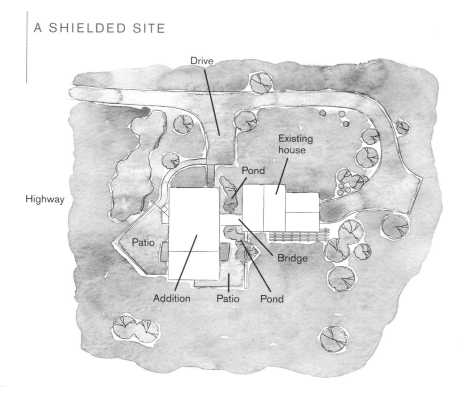

■ Notions of contemporary architecture in stone, timber, and metal are well suited to the rugged Wyoming site. The materials handle the weight of the oversize expanses of glass windows around the house. The large stone walls, heavy timber trusses, connector plates, and anchor rods also support the structure, allowing the house to withstand earthquakes and the heavy accumulations of snow the region experiences each year.

DESIGNED WITH OFFSPRING IN MIND

Martha's Vineyard, Massachusetts

City couples who dream of living in the country can still lead lives full of culture and social activity. A house designed with elegant proportions, sophisticated details, and a floor plan devoted to gracious entertaining will draw guests wherever it is located—whether it's secluded in the country, nestled into a mountaintop, or sheltered on an island.

When it came time for a husband and wife from New York City to build their dream vacation/retirement home on Martha's Vineyard, they commissioned architect Mark Simon to help them translate their desires into a perfect house for two . . . and three.

The couple presented Mark with a challenging personality profile. They described themselves as urbane and outdoorsy, literary and pragmatic, private yet socially active. Their ideal house was to be a retreat from the city for the two of them but designed so it would be a welcome place for their son and his friends to visit.

To fulfill the couple's wish list, Mark designed a main house and a

■ This shingle-clad home is long and narrow to conform to an ecologically sensitive site. Wide roof overhangs, a flared, shingled base, and rolling storm doors help shield the windowed house from fierce northeasters that blow across Martha's Vineyard.

■ The arched eyebrow window on the west side of the main house frames a second-floor study with contemplative ocean views.

137

An Open Plan

"Tightly controlled wetlands on the land limited the area where their house could be built. As a result, the floor plan is very long and narrow, and the house is only one room deep. We kept the first floor free of doors between most spaces and gathered the service rooms into two areas to allow the edges of the rest of the living spaces to remain open. Because of the long vistas on either side, the space feels bigger. Without them, the floor plan would have felt choppy."

—Mark Simon,
Centerbrook Architects

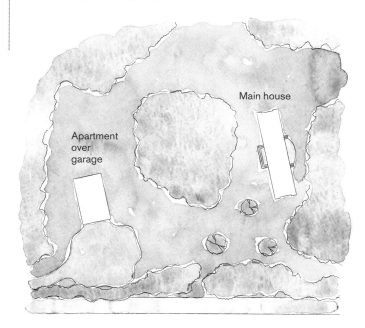

A SHARED PROPERTY

A long first-floor hallway, without doors, creates an uninterrupted view from one end of the house to the other.

separate building complete with a bachelor's pad and workshop. The family of buildings blends into its surrounding rural site, and at the same time, the design is a modern, elegant, and private solution to accommodate visiting family members.

Site Sensitive

The house is built on 10 acres of pristine marshes mixed with farmland and forest—a sanctuary from urban living. The Vineyard house is also a model of sensitivity to climate and site. Wetland setbacks posed a problem when it came time to site the buildings, so Mark designed the main house as a long, narrow, one-room-deep rectangle to fit within the tight parameters of the landscape.

The design of the 3,000-square-foot house takes advantage of nature's ample gifts. The house relies on outdoor breezes to cool down the interior during summer months. Generous roof overhangs protect the second-floor windows from the hot, penetrating sun and let the homeowners keep the windows open during summer rains, which is an important function in a house without air-conditioning.

Windows wrap around the rectangular main house to take advantage of the surrounding water views. The interior of the house is bright because it borrows so much light through all of the windows. But since the floor plan is only one room deep, Mark's challenge was to make the interior feel as spacious as possible.

A ribbon of windows wraps around the master bedroom to give the homeowners a panoramic view of the surrounding forests, fields, and water. The oversize pair of floor-to-ceiling windows (measuring 3 feet wide by 6 feet 8 inches high) is placed in the front of the house to capture the best views. The couple's master bedroom is segregated from the second-level guest room by a hallway "bridge" and is also located halfway across the property from their son's bachelor apartment.

The view from the main house to the garage/apartment is intentionally separated by a wild swath of trees, vines, and marsh grass, granting independence and privacy to both parents and grown child.

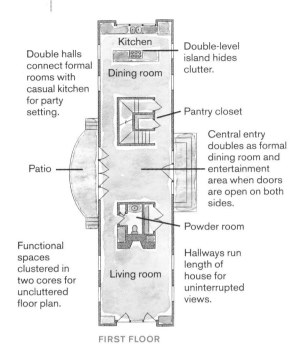

Double halls connect formal rooms with casual kitchen for party setting.

Patio

Functional spaces clustered in two cores for uncluttered floor plan.

Kitchen

Dining room

Double-level island hides clutter.

Pantry closet

Central entry doubles as formal dining room and entertainment area when doors are open on both sides.

Powder room

Living room

Hallways run length of house for uninterrupted views.

FIRST FLOOR

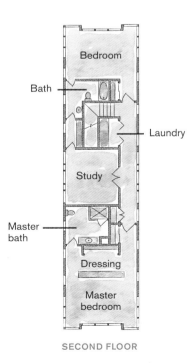

Bedroom

Bath

Laundry

Study

Master bath

Dressing

Master bedroom

SECOND FLOOR

An Open Arrangement

One way to keep living space open and flowing is to eliminate the use of doors and walls so that the rooms remain open and airy. Not only did Mark do away with doors to gain extra space, he designed hallways that run the length of the house. By creating a long and uninterrupted view from one end of the hall to the other (two halls downstairs, one hall upstairs), the viewer perceives the house to be larger than it is.

On the first floor, walls were eliminated and the powder room, fireplace, stairs, and pantry were placed into the middle of the floor plan. Placing service areas in the core area of the house diminishes barriers, creating long vistas on both sides of the house that make it feel larger.

Crossing a Bridge

The design of the second floor of the main house has more privacy in mind. Two bedrooms flank one hallway that runs the length of the house on an outer wall with windows. The floor of the hall rises up three steps in the middle to follow the curve of the eyebrow window.

The 175-square-foot kitchen is large enough for both husband and wife to cook together at the same time. The chest-high cabinet shields messy cooking activities from the living space while allowing the cooks to converse with guests.

In the living room—one of three large areas within the open plan—a heat-efficient Rumsford fireplace is encased in rough-edged, fossilized limestone. Hand-picked by one of the homeowners, it expresses her love of the natural world and offers a pleasing contrast against more refined details found elsewhere in the main house. The fireplace abuts one of two utility service cores that divide the first-floor space.

BLENDING ARCHITECTURAL INFLUENCES

The main house is a modern version of the traditional, Shingle-style house indigenous to Martha's Vineyard and Cape Cod. Mark blended several diverse architectural influences to give the house its distinguishing, almost exotic look. "Genius is hiding your sources," renowned architect Charles Moore once said. But Mark was modest enough to disclose his sources of inspiration for the house. The roof takes its cue from the Japanese Iramoya style—hipped roofs with small ventilation gables at the ends and wide overhangs—found on traditional Japanese palaces. The roof overhangs let light in but keep the rain out. The ribbon of windows recalls the designs of Frank Lloyd Wright, who also fell under the spell of Japanese style and who liked the linear look of long, connected windows. The floor plan is partially rooted in the modern ideals of architect Mies van der Rohe, who made small homes feel larger, open, and airy by keeping the kitchen and other service areas clustered in the center of the floor plan.

A 5-foot-high island counter, with china cabinets below, divides the kitchen and dining area without boxing in either space or breaking up the open first-floor plan.

The arched dormer window in the bachelor apartment replicates (on a smaller scale) the distinctive windows found in the main house.

The step up is a structural necessity to make room for the vaulted ceiling of the entry vestibule below. The step up also serves another function, acting as a bridge to separate the master bedroom from the guest room on the other side of the house. Mark designed another guest room for one very special guest—the homeowners' son—by creating a separate and private getaway just steps away from the main house.

The Bachelor's Apartment

The detached building, built especially for the couple's grown son, preserves the privacy of parents and guests. About 75 feet away from the main house, the architect built a garage with a workshop and a second-floor bachelor apartment. In the summertime—prime visiting season—the apartment is barely visible from the main house because scrub pines, wild fruit trees, vines, and marsh grasses provide a natural buffer. "The two houses are close enough to form a compound—a place for the family to reconnect," Mark says, "but they're far enough away to ensure everyone's privacy."

Mark took care to treat the apartment with the same thoughtful design as the main house. Though the building is only a total of 1,746 square feet, it resembles the main house with its matching cedar shingles, similarly styled ribbon windows, and a hipped roof with a wide overhang. The long eyebrow dormer window inside the studio apartment defines its architectural presence and character while expanding interior headroom and carving an alcove in the open space. The 686-square-foot studio apartment contains one large room with a sleeping area, small living room, kitchenette, and bath.

Together, the house and detached apartment represent one ideal living arrangement between parent and grown child. The buildings share a striking resemblance in architectural style, symmetry, orientation, proportions, and materials, though the main house is richer in its architectural references and more complex in its organization of spaces than that of the offspring. Yet both buildings have their own personalities and both function—and succeed—on their own as a retreat from city streets and island storms.

An outbuilding houses a garage, workshop, and apartment. Barn doors and an asymmetrical roof make it appear less formal than the main house. However, it retains design elements of the main house, such as the arched window and weathered shingles.

Steps lift the middle of the second-floor hallway up over the vaulted entry ceiling below. The elevated portion of the hallway also serves as a privacy bridge between the master and guest bedrooms. A pair of French doors leads to a home office.

The House They Always Wanted

"THE HUSBAND WANTED A WOOD-SHOP AND A GARAGE FOR THE CARS AND KAYAKS. THE WIFE WANTED A STUDY FOR READING AND FOR FREE-LANCE BOOK-EDITING PROJECTS. TOGETHER, THEY LONGED FOR A BIG KITCHEN WHERE BOTH OF THEM COULD COOK AND ENTERTAIN. AND AS PARENTS, THEY WANTED A STU-DIO APARTMENT FOR THEIR GROWN SON—AN INDEPENDENT SPACE THAT WOULD ENTICE HIM TO VISIT AND BRING HIS FRIENDS ALONG."

—MARK SIMON, ARCHITECT

A MODERN DESERT HOME

Scottsdale, Arizona

OPEN LAND CAN EXPAND the design possibilities for new homes. The vastness of land can inform the design of a house, as the desert did with this modern home designed for an empty-nester couple. After years spent dividing their time between New York and a weekend house on Long Island, the couple was interested in a sophisticated home that would be large enough for them and for visits from their five grown children and several grandchildren. They wanted the house, however, to have minimal impact on the surrounding Saguaro cacti and boulders.

They hired Edward Jones, an architect who is known for experimenting with building forms and materials. Edward took the couple's wish list—which included detached guest quarters, a separate master wing, and various courtyards for their grandchildren's playtime—and designed a place for them nestled in the desert.

Nature's Plan

The house was sited in the middle of the property for privacy and security, but the location accomplished several other objectives as well.

An arroyo, or dry gully, also passes through the center of the site. Planning the home around it preserved the natural drainage system and integrated

▌ Deep roof overhangs shield the large glassed-in room from the fierce Arizona sun and provide coveted shade for swimmers in the pool area located behind the house.

▌ Like the desert surrounding this retirement home, the interior has a clean, open, and unfettered sense of space. The interior walls throughout the house are simple, varnished Douglas fir.

The House We Always Wanted

"WE WANTED A HOUSE THAT WAS
ENVIRONMENTALLY CORRECT—THAT
NO MATTER WHAT ROOM WE WERE
IN WE COULD EXPERIENCE THE DESERT.
I WANTED TO BECOME PART OF THE
DESERT. WE ALSO WANTED THE
FEELING OF SEPARATION SO THAT WE
WOULD HAVE OUR OWN SPACE AND
VISITING GUESTS WOULD HAVE THEIRS."

—HOMEOWNERS

▊ A contemporary, high trellis-style wood awning, also used elsewhere around the perimeter, acts as a filter for the strong desert sunlight and serves as a porte cochere for the rear entrance of the house.

▊ Rammed-earth walls, like the one that encloses the garage areas, are naturalistic backdrops for the boulders, Saguaro cacti, and other desert flora around which the house was designed.

the rugged beauty of the land into the design. The house was also planned around the preservation of a 125-year-old Palo Verde tree, which borders a garage wall.

In contrast to neighboring mansions, the 7,800-square-foot house, though large, has a low profile because it sits hunkered down on the landscape rather than trying to compete against it. Working carefully around native flora and boulders also helped the house blend into the landscape and appear smaller than its square footage might suggest.

The house is a compound of separate wings used for differing functions. Each wing relates visually and spatially to the entire structure and to the surrounding desert with a series of outdoor connectors such as walkways, patios, gardens, and courtyards. "These connectors are about the house acknowledging where it is," says Edward. "The natural forces of the site determined the layout, even the materials, but the house invented itself, and that defines architecture."

Spanish Inspiration

Compounds are ideal for uniting large families on common ground, while recognizing the mutual independence of grown children and their parents.

The main house in the compound contains a wide-open living and entertaining space with entry hall, kitchen and breakfast area, living and

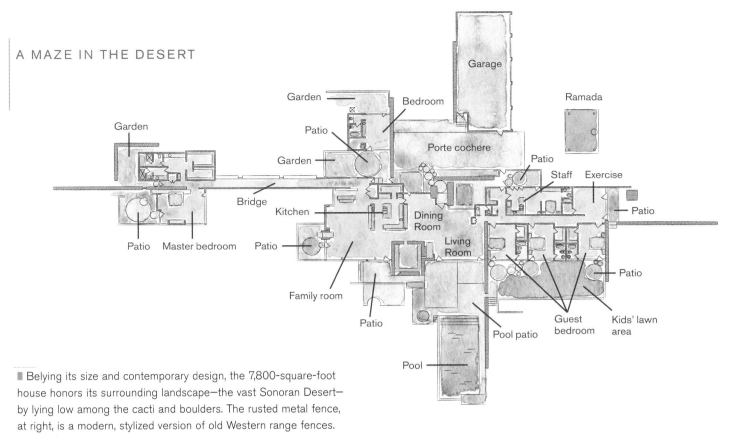

Garden

Bedroom

Garage

Ramada

Patio

Garden

Porte cochere

Patio

Garden

Garden

Staff

Exercise

Bridge

Kitchen

Patio

Dining Room

Patio

Patio

Patio

Master bedroom

Patio

Living Room

Family room

Patio

Patio

Patio

Pool patio

Guest bedroom

Kids' lawn area

Pool

▌ Belying its size and contemporary design, the 7,800-square-foot house honors its surrounding landscape—the vast Sonoran Desert— by lying low among the cacti and boulders. The rusted metal fence, at right, is a modern, stylized version of old Western range fences.

In the main house, kitchen cabinets and half walls divide the living and entertaining spaces from the kitchen and still keep the floor plan open. The narrow opening on the right leads to the husband's office—a cave-like, 12-foot cube enclosed by rammed-earth walls. Rather than flood the house with full sunlight, the light seeps in through an 8-inch-wide skylight running the length of the ridge in the ceiling. The ridge is edged with silver leafing to diffuse the light.

dining rooms, and a family room with bar and sitting area. Off the latter area is a guest wing that houses three bedrooms, a house staff's apartment and laundry room, and a fitness room with sauna. A courtyard off the kitchen leads to a single guest-bedroom wing bordered by private gardens.

The entry side of the main house consists of a four-bay garage outfitted with hydraulic lifts to double the car-storage capacity. The open ramada (an open porch or arbor), used to wash cars, and a high porte cochere (a covered approach to a house large enough for vehicles to pull up to the front entrance), with a slatted wood covering to filter the strong sunlight, are both inspired by Spanish architecture.

A Master-Suite Pavilion

Despite the number of guest rooms, this is meant to be a retired couple's house. To emphasize the point, the master-bedroom suite occupies a separate pavilion, which is located 120 feet away from the guest quarters. In addition, as if to underscore their desire for privacy, the pavilion sits on the far side of the gully that splits the property.

The suite is a small, separate, and intimate house (a total of 800 square feet), with 180-degree views of the desert. It's reached by an enclosed bridge—a hallway that floats above the gully—and is lined with windows on the north wall and, on the south, a black carpet-covered wall for hanging family portraits. Automated blackout curtains are closed to block the sun from the master bedroom but are opened at night so the couple can enjoy brilliant views of the city lights in Scottsdale, 20 miles away. To keep the pavilion in scale with its surroundings and because it would be visible in so much open space, the structure is semienclosed by a garden with a patio and fountain, inside an envelope of thick, rammed-earth walls.

Private Places

Large, well-designed homes with open plans carve smaller areas out of the floor plan for retreat, reflection, or work. The retreat in this desert house is a 12-foot cube cut partway into the wall of the main living area and jutting

A family room and sitting area in the main wing looks out to a patio and the desert in the distance. Most of the interior spaces lead to outdoor rooms of smaller scale and greater privacy to contrast with the large, open floor plan of the house and the vastness of the surrounding desert.

Partial walls help to divide the space and separate functions without blocking light from filtering into the rooms. The varying wall heights also diminish the expansive, open nature of the interior.

A 60-foot-long hallway bridges an outdoor gully and separates the master-bedroom wing from the rest of the compound. While the northern-facing wall is open to sweeping views, the southern-facing wall is lined with carpeting for mounting family portraits. Small stained-glass windows in the space diffuse the intense desert light.

halfway out into the rear patio. Used as the husband's office, it is a cavelike space, surrounded by 3-foot- to 4-foot-thick rammed-earth walls and accessed by small openings in the front and back of the room. Cool, enveloping, and seemingly far removed from the desert, as well as from the rest of the home, the office is nonetheless close to modern conveniences and pleasures: the kitchen and refrigerator, living room and television, the front entry, the patio, and, of course, the pool.

Other private places are discovered outside. The house was designed as a single level of projecting and receding walls, so wherever an inhabitable interior area exists, a corresponding inhabitable exterior space is found.

One such private exterior space is the long courtyard of thick lawn behind the three guest bedrooms. Lawns don't belong in the desert, the architect maintains, and they're rarely found in a Jones-designed house. In this case, however, the space presented itself as a natural, private courtyard and an oasis for the owners' grandchildren and dogs—a rectangle of greenery enclosed by concrete-block walls—without intruding upon the desert. A narrow opening between long sections of wall leads to the pool.

▌ Every room in this desert house has a corresponding outdoor room, such as the patio off one of the guest bedrooms. The pool is located on the other side of the rammed-earth wall, shown on the right.

Rammed-Earth Walls

The compound is encircled with thick, energy-efficient, rammed-earth walls, which were erected on-site. The moistened earth was mixed with small amounts of cement, then packed into wooden forms to create the 18-inch-thick walls. (It became not only the first rammed-earth house to be built in Scottsdale but also the first one for the architect.)

These earthen surfaces look natural against the rusted metal siding and corrugated-metal roofs chosen for the exterior. As on other new houses out West designed with metal details, the use of metal recalls old barns and home-steads, but it is also practical in this climate because it can tolerate the 115°F heat.

On the inside, the walls are finished with a clear, water-repellent sealer. The sealer not only preserves the walls and helps keep the fine-grained earth intact but also gives the walls a sheen more in keeping with the interior surfaces of plaster, varnished Douglas fir, and sand-blasted glass.

Rather than allow the scorching rays of the sun to flood the interior, the house is designed to help filter the strong desert sun. In the main wing, sunlight enters through an 8-inch-wide skylight that runs the length of the ridge. In order to extract the most light from this long sliver, the northern edge of the ridge opening is lined with silver leaf. Though the material is functional because it reflects and diffuses sunlight without bringing in the heat, this expensive but breathtaking silver-leaf detailing is also aesthetically pleasing—an appropriate finish for the home of a retired jeweler.

 The structure that houses the master suite is located 120 feet away from the guest wing, across a craggy gully. Architect Edward Jones designed the bed, night table, and bookcases. From behind the bed, a rammed-earth wall continues out into the landscape as a way to tie together the indoor/outdoor spaces.

Visible from the entry and on the far side of the house, the negative-edge pool sits 8 feet above the ground and shimmers like a mirage above the desert floor. Another rammed-earth wall separates the children's and grandchildren's wing from the owners' outdoor entertaining area, creating a toasty sundeck on one side and a shady refuge on the other.

The exterior of the guest-bedroom wing is a natural oasis, finished with grass, for the owners' grandchildren. A concrete-block wall keeps the lawn in and the desert out.

ARCHITECT'S NOTES

Secret Spaces

"The Arizona climate seems to insist that homes have outdoor living spaces. The perimeter of this house creates outdoor spaces that are private, intimate, and rather secret. In fact, every habitable interior space has an adjacent exterior room, which one discovers when [one] moves around and through the house. For example, the main entrance is found inside the cavelike masses of rammed-earth monoliths, and the raised garden patio between the guest house and the main home can only be discovered after passage through another interim space."
—Edward Jones, Jones Studio Inc.

A Family Compound
Spreads Out

Martha's Vineyard, Massachusetts

When people with children from previous marriages come together later in life, the union produces an opportunity to create a larger nest for the combined, extended family. That's just how one couple decided to handle vacationing with their large brood.

The couple, who originally lived in a charming cottage overlooking the harbor, couldn't imagine living anywhere else. They had a sizable problem, however: Together they had six children, each of whom had young children of their own. Although the various sets of kids and grandkids took turns visiting because of the cottage's limited accommodations, the couple knew that everyone enjoyed being together at the same time. But solving the problem by expanding the house was not possible due to the island's strict waterfront building regulations.

Rather than stay in the cottage, the couple moved six houses away and hired architects Mark Hutker and Phil Regan to renovate three small, Shingle-style bungalows that were sprawled across the two-acre waterfront property. First, the architects renovated the buildings, creating suites of bedrooms that allowed the clan to ebb and flow in and out of the compound with the weekend and holiday tides. The main cottage was designed to make it the social epicenter of the com-

■ A compound on the harbor, part of a 1906 estate, was renovated to fit a large family that frequently reunites. In the main cottage living room (right), walls were stripped of four layers of paint, then restored to the original quartersawn oak paneling. Rare Rookwood Pottery tiles were also restored and reset around the fireplace.

Refurbished carriage house doors slide open to reveal a combined exterior/interior hallway and two bedrooms located in the guest house closest to the road.

pound. Finally, a hideaway master-bedroom suite for the homeowners transformed the second floor of the main cottage, the last touch needed to address each of the family members' needs.

Seven Guest Rooms

The renovation created seven guest bedrooms out of the original outbuildings. The carriage house, closest to the beach road, was originally a two-car garage and a chauffeur's small apartment. In disrepair, those quarters were gutted and the space converted to a comfortable living room with a wood-burning stove, kitchen, and bath. On the other side of the 900-square-foot building, two new bedrooms displaced the bays. The bedrooms are accessible through separate sets of French doors that open from a narrow breeze-way running inside the original, reconditioned, sliding garage doors. Now, cars park in the broad, pebbled courtyard, which doubles as an open-air entry foyer for the compound.

Seventy-five feet to the west, up a new slate path that crosses the lawn, a 400-square-foot outbuilding that was once used as a casino and bathhouse

A broad path connects the guest carriage house, at right, to the homeowner's cottage in the background, overlooking the water.

▌ What once housed a casino on the original estate became a one-bedroom guest house. The smallest of the three buildings on the property, it is a quick walk from the main house's porch (in the foreground), located 60 feet away.

Historic Connections

"Our biggest job was to connect the house to [the] waterfront and to the natural light and breezes without losing a sense of the historic[al] context. We altered the existing fabric, but we left a trail of shadows—lines between old and new flooring and doorway—so in the future, a knowledgeable architect can follow them and restore the house to its original floor plan if necessary."

—Mark Hutker,
Mark Hutker and Associates Architects

The stone path leads up to the heart of the couple's compound, which is the parents' cottage, a completely renovated and expanded bungalow.

MAIN HOUSE RENOVATION

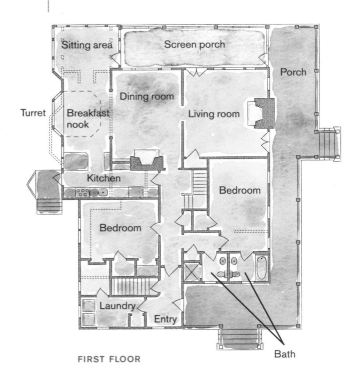

FIRST FLOOR

has become a one-bedroom apartment, with a modernized bath, kitchenette, and hardwood floor replacing the old decking. South of the casino, as the family calls the building, is a larger renovated beach house and guest house with a substantially altered floor plan. Two first-floor guest bedrooms have been gained in the process.

Instead of stacking all of the beds in one place, the arrangement created three separate groupings of rooms—suites within the compound—to serve the multiple needs of the family.

Redefining a Cottage's Role

For the most part, the architects who designed early-19th-century houses on the East Coast were more concerned about constructing simple, durable shelters than they were about whether picture windows should be included for a view to the water. Historically, most houses on this island focused on the interior rooms, which were defined solely by function, not aesthetics.

This was particularly true of cottages built in 1906 as ancillary outbuildings, and it held true for the main cottage in this compound—a 3,000-square-foot, Shingle-style bungalow—which is located directly on the harbor. The original porch wrapped around three sides of the building, protecting the interior from the site as much as connecting to it.

The parents' porch wraps around the main house on three sides and leads out to a private pier on the water off Martha's Vineyard. The porch also connects the house with the site.

Now, nearly a century later, the buildings' unified purpose was to draw a big, extended family together, with the parents' main cottage serving as the focal point—the apex of the triangle drawn by the three buildings—and social center of the compound.

Repositioned Rooms

The cottage's original floor plan consisted of a warren of rooms. Expanded and realigned doorways help rooms flow into one another and make the spaces in the main house more appropriate for socializing. The removal of walls also helped reposition rooms. The old kitchen in the back of the house was converted into one of the first-floor guest bedrooms, while the pantry and an enclosed porch became the new, enlarged, updated kitchen.

A one-and-a-half-story turret with a cathedral ceiling and an upper bank of clerestory windows altered one wall of the cottage. Though it only bumps the wall out by 4 feet, the turret creates an eat-in breakfast bay off the new kitchen and brings natural light into the adjoining dining room

SECOND FLOOR

Deck

Attic space

Master bedroom

Dressing area

Bedroom

Attic space

Bath

Attic space

■ The addition of an 18-foot-wide dormer on the east side of the main house turned a dark, attic-like room into a master bedroom with private deck and sweeping overviews of the harbor. An antique chest, partially visible at the foot of the bed, opens by remote control and raises a sunken television.

that is located deep inside the house. With a total seating capacity of 22, the combined eat-in area and dining room form the core of the compound's central gathering area.

Hideaway Master Suite

Even with the addition of the independent guest houses, the couple decided they needed a place of their own, far from the family. Their hideaway was designed on the second floor of the main house.

In the 1960s, the addition of a small shed dormer tacked onto the hipped roof created enough headroom for a small bedroom. But the floor was dark and stuffy like a typical attic. To create an ideal suite for the parents, it was decided that the space would be one of the only areas in the compound that would be designed as a completely new space, which turned out to be a radical departure from the structure of the original room.

The shed dormer was removed, and four hipped dormers of varying widths were cut into the roof slopes. The dormers, which fall within the

The addition of the one-and-a-half-story turret enhances the eat-in breakfast area. The upper clerestory windows bring light through the bay and into the dining room, which is situated deep inside the floor plan.

RECLAIMED MATERIALS

n general, building on Martha's Vineyard is thoughtful and site sensitive because New England architects and homeowners on the island are generally reticent about expressing their wealth or their wares. Mark's renovation of the compound follows suit.

The three buildings were re-sided but with the same cedar shakes as before. Otherwise, Mark made use of existing materials wherever possible. In the living room of the main cottage, for instance, four layers of lemon-color paint were removed from the original quartersawn oak paneling, and the wood was restored. Oak trim reclaimed from elsewhere in the house frames the new picture windows so that they blend with existing double-hung windows. Newly painted trim distinguishes it from the original trim and casts light back into the interior. Restored Craftsman-era Rookwood Pottery tiles, now valued as collectibles, frame the fireplace.

Restored oak paneling surrounds the doorways in the main cottage. The doors were widened and realigned for through-views and increased sunlight between rooms.

▮ Combining a former pantry and an enclosed porch created a larger, much brighter kitchen, located in the front of the main house rather than in the back, as before. The kitchen looks old, but it is convenient and efficient. The porcelain British butler's sink, set against the back wall, gets ample use as a lobster-holding sink.

▮ The eat-in breakfast area floats between the kitchen and dining room and overlooks lush English gardens. The addition of the one-and-a-half-story turret brought this section of the house to life.

building's historical and architectural context, opened up the ceilings to create a large master bedroom, window seat, and terrace on one side of the house and created room for a master bath on the opposite side. An antique tub installed in the dormer was raised to window level to give the homeowners a relaxing and private view outside.

With floor space at a premium on this level, the long walkway between the master bed and bath became a combination walk-through closet and dressing room. A series of closets lines one side of the hall, a wall of built-in drawers the other. Because the hall is far from the dormers, skylights were installed to illuminate the area.

For now, every child, grandchild, and grandparent has a place to sleep when visiting the island. The owners, who from the beginning envisioned the compound as a family gathering spot as opposed to a vacation/retirement home, are hoping that it will continue to be a meeting place for generations to come.

A porch on the main cottage overlooks the water and becomes a quiet time-out area for the homeowners after a busy day gathered together with their clan.

FROM CRAMPED TO COMFORTABLE

Bay Area, California

ONCE THE CHILDREN LEAVE HOME, there's suddenly more room in the house than two people really need, but it's seldom the type of space a couple wants. For one couple who decided to stay in their family home, extra space was the problem, and the solution was to rearrange and renovate rooms to serve their evolving needs.

Jim and Denny Hoelter raised three children in a 2,000-square-foot turn-of-the-century estate cottage, which they bought in 1970. Once the children left home, the house felt too big. The couple decided to look for another place to live. They wanted to stay in the community, so they began looking at local houses and building lots before realizing that the best idea was to stay and remodel their house. But the redwood-sided cottage felt cramped, the original kitchen was particularly small and dark, and the front entrance was difficult to find.

When the couple first contacted architect John Malick, all they had in mind was a remodel of their kitchen into a large, sunlit area, with access to the garden,

■ The breakfast room, with a new cathedral ceiling, extended the original footprint of the house by just 8 feet, but it gives Jim and Denny a bright, casual, open space large enough to accommodate the entire family during visits.

■ Adding banks of windows, trellises, and classic landscaping completely transformed a turn-of-the-century cottage.

A soaring ceiling and transom windows make this bright kitchen the couple's favorite room. The cabinets are crafted from simple Douglas fir.

The House We Always Wanted

"WE DIDN'T WANT TO LIVE IN A BIG HOUSE NOW THAT KIDS ARE GONE, BUT WE DID WANT A KITCHEN THAT WAS LARGE ENOUGH TO LIVE IN AND ONE THAT OPENED UP INTO THE GARDEN. WHAT WE WANTED TO GAIN WAS LIGHT AND BRIGHTNESS INSIDE THE HOUSE. THAT'S ALL WE WERE ASKING FOR. BUT JOHN MALICK HAS A GREAT IMAGINATION, AND HE TRANSFORMED AND OPENED UP THE WHOLE HOUSE."

—DENNY HOELTER, HOMEOWNER

The overscaled front door—it's 4½ feet wide and 2 inches thick—is repositioned from the side of the house. The trellises and gardens are inspired by drawings of Beatrix Ferand, a California landscape architect.

where they could be comfortable with one another and with their visiting children and grandchildren. Once they visualized the transformation of the kitchen, the couple decided to renovate the entire house in a contemporary Craftsman style.

John retained the warmth, coziness, and human scale of traditional Craftsman houses while opening up the interior walls and ceilings. The renovation not only turned the crowded cottage into a spacious and updated new home, it created a house that entices children and grandchildren to visit.

Reallocating Space

To start the renovation, Jim and Denny examined their needs and took the time to decide how to reallocate existing space in their home. Since their children live close by, they decided to focus on rooms that serve adults, whether it's just the two of them using the room or the extended family over for a visit.

Seeing an existing space in a fresh, new way is part of the process of living in "the house to ourselves." In this renovation, the first-floor master bedroom became the new kitchen to take advantage of daylong sunlight and access to existing gardens. A new master bedroom was added to the second floor, and the original, dark, confined kitchen became a mudroom and a bathroom.

The addition of new rooms included a formal entry with a widened front door; a breakfast room off the kitchen; and a large master bedroom located over the living room, with an adjoining office for Denny. Trellises, terraces, gardens, and footpaths wrap around the front and sides of the house to connect all the rooms to one another.

To rearrange rooms, John matched function and location to maximize light and views. It made sense to move the kitchen from the shaded rear of the house to the sunnier front corner of the house, which has access to the garden.

Multiple Interior Levels

Although the original footprint was expanded by just 8 feet, the house grew from 2,000 square feet to nearly 3,200 square feet. The new space not only gave Jim and Denny the kinds of rooms they wanted but also permitted the entire interior to be divided into areas that are both open and comfortably scaled. This is achieved, in part, by the use of multiple levels.

In the new layout, the living room drops down three steps from the main level, creating a 10-foot-high room that's a retreat from the rest of the house. The space remains visually connected by a hallway to the main, atrium-style staircase. Over the living room, the new master bedroom sits three steps above the second-floor hallway, a visual way to signal to others that this is a very private place in the house for the homeowners to enjoy.

The house is further subdivided by several other room reorganizations. The living room, staircase hall, and Jim's office comprise one wing of the house at ground level. At the other end, across the entry foyer, the kitchen wing contains six rooms of varying sizes: breakfast room, kitchen, kitchen terrace, pantry, half bath, and mudroom. Doors in the central foyer can close off both ends from one another, if necessary, so that Jim and Denny

A sandstone tile–faced fireplace complements the wood walls and adds warmth to the large room, even when a fire isn't burning. Sconces in the exposed rafter tails softly light the ceiling. Stairs allowed the height of the sunken living room to expand to 10 feet.

Jim's office, designed to look like something between an office and a room in a men's club, is located in what used to be the kitchen. Douglas fir cabinets and bookcases line three walls. The room also is outfitted with an exhaust fan for Jim's cigar smoke.

are able to enjoy smaller, more intimate scales of living within the large, handcrafted structure.

Contemporary Craftsman Style

The renovated house generally follows classic Craftsman design, which revels in wood, handcraftsmanship, and an abundance of cozy nooks. John adapted the style, however, because the couple wanted more indoor natural light. Jim and Denny were ready to upgrade materials throughout the house, so John took the best features of Craftsman houses and created a fine crafted home with a bright interior.

A forest of vertical-grain, Douglas fir paneling, wainscoting, and casework sheathes much of the first floor. In the living room, hollowed rafter ends accommodate sconces that bathe the ceiling in a soft glow of light during the evening. High above the second-floor landing, clerestory windows draw sunlight deep into the stairwell.

What marks the difference between "before" and "after" here is the alignment of long, shallow rooms along the front of the renovated house, with walls filled by an abundance of French doors and casement and transom windows; in the original cottage, the rooms tended to be deep, dark, and tunnel-like.

A MAGICAL REALM FOR GRANDKIDS

Though the family cottage is designed mainly for grown-ups, it preserves the spirit of childhood play for visiting grandchildren. The former pantry, located under the stairs, has become a little playroom—more like a magical, hidden realm in the house—and it's the one space in the renovation that was left untouched by the architect's hand.

The small arched door to the playroom—original to the cottage—was stripped of paint. In contrast to the rest of the house, the old pine paneling inside the room was left unfinished so that the children would feel free to draw and scribble on the walls. The playroom is furnished with toys and other items the owners' own children used to play with when they were little: a child-size table and chairs, a play sink and stove, a cabinet for doll dishes, and a doll bed and dresser.

The old pantry, with its original arched door stripped of paint, makes a perfect clubhouse under the stairs for the couple's visiting grandchildren.

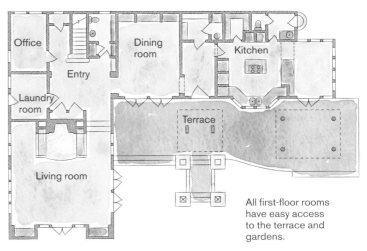

All first-floor rooms have easy access to the terrace and gardens.

FIRST FLOOR

Office

Dining room

Kitchen

Entry

Laundry room

Terrace

Living room

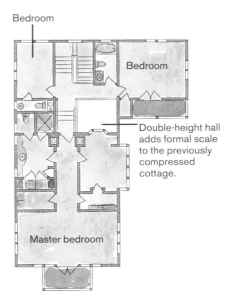

Bedroom

Bedroom

Master bedroom

Double-height hall adds formal scale to the previously compressed cottage.

SECOND FLOOR

▌ A love of Craftsman design inspired this house, and the influence of Japanese temples on the California Craftsman style is apparent in the hallway. The wood is finished with a natural Cabot stain, cut with a 50 percent solution of white pigment. Multiple sources of lighting from elsewhere in the house further brighten the space.

A skylight above the second-floor staircase landing highlights the fine wood and wrought-iron work in the hallway. Denny's office, with an interior bay window, is located to the left.

An ideal mix of classic and contemporary in the house is achieved in the second-floor master bedroom. The beamed and raftered cathedral ceiling and the three walls of windows possess a formality and solidity usually found in older houses. The surfaces are painted white—which instantly modernizes the character of the room—with the light from all the glass bouncing off the ceiling rather than being absorbed by it. In the front of the master bedroom, French doors lead to a terrace overlooking the gardens.

Jim and Denny's renovated cottage is still considered to be the family home, but it's unrecognizable from the "before" photos. Changes in the couple's lifestyle created a new map for living, which was overlaid on the old house. Where spaces were once cramped and dark, they are now open and light filled. Where once everyone was crowded together, now there is room enough for the couple to have the house to themselves while sharing it with family and friends, too.

After living in the house nearly 30 years and raising three children there, Jim and Denny completely renovated and restyled their cramped and dark 1906 cottage. They added a master-bedroom suite with a balcony over the living room and a network of trellises and arbors across the front of the Craftsman-style house.

Denny studies genealogy in this large office next to the master-bedroom suite. The office receives daylong sunlight and has views to the front walk. Drawers under the window seat were custom-made to fit her genealogical charts.

■ By adding onto the second floor, architect John Malick was able to give the owners a soaring master-bedroom suite with a balcony overlooking the gardens. The 2-foot-wide wooden eaves protect the balcony from bad weather but are shallow enough to let light into the bedroom.

PART FOUR

Pursuing Our Passions

The House as Office, Studio, and Workshop

TIME FOR A CHANGE

THIS REMARKABLE TRANSFORMATION of an ordinary 1960s builders' Colonial began with the purchase of a new refrigerator. When the old one quit working, the owners thought that as long as they were buying a new model, they might as well redo the kitchen. But once they started thinking about a new kitchen, they took a good look at the rest of the house and realized, after living 25 years in the place, how much they disliked it.

Like many couples, they simply hadn't had the time or energy to consider making changes before. Both professionals— she was a psychiatrist, he a surgeon—they raised two children in the 2,400-square-foot Dutch Colonial without giving much thought to the things that bothered them. Two front doors on opposite sides of the house led visitors astray more often than not, and once inside, they found themselves in dark hallways that led to a series of small, enclosed rooms.

All the while, the couple's interests in collecting art and antique clocks had blossomed into passionate hobbies. By the time the children left home, the wife was stacking paintings against the walls and the husband was restoring the clocks in the living room.

Yet they didn't want to move. They love the neighborhood and the property—a little over an acre of private land, high on

▮ Visitors used to have trouble finding the front door and, once inside, an even harder time reaching the home's social spaces. A new vestibule—with a salvaged door, sidelights, and glazed pediments—welcomes guests and properly introduces them to the character of the redesigned interior.

▮ The new formal front entrance goes out of its way to beckon visitors, and it clearly delineates the way in and out. The addition of the entry, with all its windows, also brings ample light into the living room and front hall.

It's difficult to believe that the original family house turned into this remarkable remodel of a builders' Colonial. The homeowners' current lives bear little resemblance to the lives they had when they raised their children, so they let their passions and pursuits inform the redesign of the house.

The porch light, handcrafted by the homeowner, reflects the passion that empty nesters can bring to hobbies, and ultimately to their homes.

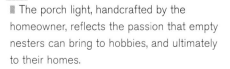

a hill at the end of a suburban street. Although their children live across the country, most of their valuable social and professional relationships remain close by. Besides, the wife has invested a good deal of time over the years in her perennial gardens behind the house. When the couple retired two years ago, they suddenly had the time, the energy, and the resources to live exactly the way they wanted.

As a result, an average, partitioned family house was transformed into a new, slightly larger "palace" of open space filled with natural light for a couple who wound up finding their place as empty nesters right in their own backyard.

Reinventing the House

Architect Craig Saunders's remodeling plan called for nothing less than a reinvention of the entire house, without adding much space to the original square footage. The couple didn't need more space—in fact, they had more than enough room for the two of them.

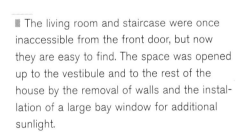

A FLOOR PLAN TRANSFORMED

Double-height sunroom

Circular garden wall connects yard to the house.

Terrace

Dining room

Kitchen

Family room

Hall

Clock tower

Living room

Entry

Light well

FIRST FLOOR

▮ The living room and staircase were once inaccessible from the front door, but now they are easy to find. The space was opened up to the vestibule and to the rest of the house by the removal of walls and the installation of a large bay window for additional sunlight.

French doors in the guest room open into the clock tower. Handcrafted wood window screens help filter morning light.

From his woodworking shop in the basement, the husband designed and built this sycamore-veneer desk, inlaid with maple burl and ebony, and a matching chair for his wife's office, which was formerly a child's bedroom. The French doors also open into the clock tower.

Like so many other empty nesters, they just needed rooms that served their individual purposes.

Craig changed three things in the house to open it up. First, he added a clearly defined formal entrance and, as a result, reoriented the house to the site. Second, Craig opened up rooms to one another and to the sun and outdoors. And, third, he created soaring new spaces with room devoted to the couple's pursuit of their passions.

The simplest part of the plan called for pulling down interior walls that subdivided the first floor. Immediately, the rooms opened up to one another, but they didn't truly breathe with new life until sections of the exterior walls were broken through for three small additions.

Today, the house is only 800 square feet larger than the original floor plan. Yet because the new spaces have high ceilings and are surrounded by glass, they give the sensation and appearance of doubling the size of the original house. This feat is also accomplished with varying the heights of ceilings throughout the house and by aligning doorways and windows so that most rooms have glimpses of other rooms from within the house.

■ The husband's office, filled with handmade furniture and pieces from the couple's art collection, looks out to the two-story conservatory and gardens beyond—views unimaginable in the original house.

■ ARCHITECT'S NOTES

Marrying Old with New

"The challenge was to take a series of little isolated boxes and open them up to create a suitable stage for the antique clocks and the paintings the couple had collected over the years. We used the clock tower in front of the house and the sunroom in the rear not only to showcase the collections but also to create a sense of transitional space between the inside and the outside. Sunlight that pours in from both additions infiltrates the middle of what used to be a very dark house."

—Craig Saunders,
Du Bose Associates, Inc., Architects

A Welcoming Entryway

Older suburban houses typically don't focus on the entryway but are usually oriented toward the garage. The remodel of this house now includes a formal front entrance to greet guests.

"It was impossible to tell where you were supposed to enter the house," Craig says of the former front entries. "Both were identical, both were dark and unwelcoming. We wanted to tell people how to get into the house, and we wanted to lift the entrance up so you weren't in a low, dark space once you entered."

A portico and 100-square-foot vestibule were added to the northwest corner of the house. Rather than having to search for the entry, guests can find the front door easily—the steps and solid railings angling out to them like outstretched arms. The overhang is pitched low, leaving enough room for glassed-in pediments. The door was salvaged from an older building. But this vestibule does more than act as a transitional space. It introduces the house and offers visitors several options of where to head so they don't feel trapped in a small hallway.

Once in the house, it's hard to miss the clock-tower addition, a homage to the couple's passion for art and antique clocks.

Celebrating Time and Space

Craig added two double-height spaces to bring natural light into the house. The height of a two-story clock tower balances the height of the

■ The two-and-a-half-story tower showcases the couple's extensive antique clock collection. The tower also acts as a skylight to bring sunlight directly into the living room. Balconies off the tower connect to his and her offices on the second floor and give the couple visual access to their treasures.

The House
They Always Wanted

ONCE THEIR CHILDREN MOVED OUT
OF THE HOUSE, THE HOMEOWNERS
HAD MORE THAN ENOUGH ROOM FOR
THEMSELVES. BUT THEY WANTED TO
OPEN UP THE DARK HOUSE WITH
NATURAL LIGHT, ADD WINDOWS OUT
TO THE REAR GARDENS, CREATE
HIS AND HER OFFICES WITH VIEWS
INTO OTHER ROOMS, AND HAVE THE
INTERIOR SERVE AS A BACKDROP FOR
THEIR COLLECTION OF ARTWORK
AND ANTIQUE CLOCKS.

conservatory and makes the remodeling project appear well thought out and executed.

Though a clock tower is a bold move to add on to a 50-year-old Colonial, it is an instance of an architect thinking outside the box. Craig's idea for a clock tower speaks more to the clients' desires and interests and less about the typical way Colonials are remodeled. Designed to showcase the couple's antique clock collection, Craig created the tower to have the stature and bearing of a grandfather clock. The two-and-a-half-story addition, occupying just 81 square feet, allows the clocks to be seen from a number of different rooms, and it doubles as a bountiful well of light that pours into both floors of the house.

A 20-foot-high conservatory was added at the back of the house, off the opened kitchen, and completes the remodel. A second-floor guest room and the husband's and wife's separate offices feature French doors and narrow balconies that open into both the clock tower and the conservatory. Along with the clock tower, the conservatory also infuses the upstairs with natural light and ventilation.

Anchoring the House

To help settle the remodel into its mature and hilly landscape, a curving deck was added to the exterior. The Colonial always appeared to be perched precariously on its lot. "As you approached the house, it always seemed as if it were going to come sliding down the hill toward you," Craig says.

The deck does a number of things to balance the house. It wraps the clock tower and the front of the house, much like a ship's deck, and gives the impression of the house riding the swells of the site. The deck also serves as an outdoor living room and visually connects the conservatory in front to the terrace in back.

This remodel is far from a perfect marriage of old and new, traditional and contemporary. It is simply its own house, indigenous to the architect's imagination and expressive of the owners' tastes and needs.

▌ A two-story conservatory added to the back of the house opens into the kitchen and the husband's second-story office, above. The conservatory also answers a wish the couple had to have access to their backyard gardens. The deck wraps around the side and back of the house.

■ The kitchen and one of the home offices overlook the two-story conservatory. In their past life, the couple ate in a dark, enclosed kitchen or in the formal dining room. Now they take all their meals in the conservatory, which is flooded with light throughout the day. The space is graced by an early-20th-century work by New England portrait painter Robert MacCameron.

A WEAVER AND
WOODCUTTER'S REFUGE

Chatham County, North Carolina

ACADEMIC LIFESTYLE resembles suburban lifestyle in one respect: The housing is homogeneous, designed alike for affordability and planned around a common sense of identity that the builders assume the homeowners will share. There usually comes a time for academicians and suburbanites to want to live in a home that enables them to express their creative passions and interests. It was at this point when David and Judith, having raised two sons in a faculty house on the Duke University campus in Durham, North Carolina, went looking at property for a new home.

When they found what they were looking for—a 200-year-old cabin and over 90 acres of rural timberland a handful of miles south of Durham—they hired architect Scott Neeley to turn the property into their retirement getaway. Scott renovated the cabin for use as a guest house and designed a 3,500-square-foot contemporary farmhouse just for the couple. Judith is a weaver and wanted a light-filled studio. David, retired from teaching and consult-

■ The two-story weaving studio sits prominently in front of the house, where it catches morning light. From the second-story loft, Judith can see out to the main road and the 200-year-old guest cabin on the property. To the far left is the studio's private porch.

■ The entry gallery, filled with books and collectibles, connects the kitchen, dining room (straight ahead), and the couple's workspaces to the master bedroom and exercise-room wing. To the right, French doors lead straight through to an inner courtyard.

■ The U-shaped plan allows for more windows to be installed in each room, resulting in more natural light streaming in from outside. The shape of the house also helps separate private and public spaces.

■ The 1-foot-wide by 6-foot-long spruce boards that clad the studio porch are painted gray to distinguish the space from the rest of the house, which has horizontal siding.

ing, farms timber on the land and needed an office and study from which to manage his new career.

The house they had in mind would also be designed in such a way that it would be able to support the community of artists and craftspeople among whom they wanted to live. It would respect the rural region while defining the couple's place in its context. Judith also wanted the design of the house to take advantage of the surrounding wooded views while maintaining a central, private space in the middle of it all.

A Courtyard Plan

It's not surprising that so many empty nesters envision courtyards when planning their retirement home. Although most couples remain actively involved in family, hobbies, volunteer work, or new careers, this is also the time of life for inward reflection and periodic sanctuary from the outer world.

Scott designed the couple's house in a U shape—two single-level wings, connected by a gallery hall—enclosing a garden courtyard. In front of the wings are twin towers, one containing Judith's two-story studio and the other a garage and second-floor guest room.

The courtyard plan creates an oasis of privacy and order in the middle of the forest, while allowing light to penetrate rooms on all sides. But it also separates the public and private spaces in a clearly defined way. Family homes divide these spaces, too, but usually by isolating them from one another. In

■ These handsome kitchen cabinets, made by a local cabinetmaker, feature homegrown walnut doors with reeded (or fluted) glass and maple countertops. David created a computer program to design the backsplash tiles in a random pattern.

■ Though the breakfast area is small and cozy, a high ceiling and wall of windows makes the modest nook feel palatial. A stained-glass window adds a touch of color to the serene kitchen.

this house, counters and built-in furniture indoors and a courtyard outdoors separate the lower-level rooms from each other. The divisions separate the spaces while the homeowners are able to see from one space into the other.

Both wings of the house have access to the central courtyard. They're also linked by the front gallery—an 8-foot-wide, light-filled hallway open at either end. Despite the fact that the public area is a single space with a soaring ceiling, it is divided by low, freestanding dividers that double as storage cabinets and look like fine, handmade furniture. A further subdivision occurs at the end of the living room, where bookcases and a lowered ceiling create an intimate fireplace nook that contrasts with the open main room.

A Private Studio and Study

For a husband and wife who have divergent passions and projects, individual workspaces became a priority. With the children grown and Judith's career as a housewife changed, the couple decided to emphasize Judith's passion for weaving in the design of the house, and that wish helped to define the two-story studio in the new home.

The first floor of the studio is filled with a wooden spinning wheel and loom and a wall of cubbyholes filled with silk and wool. The handcrafted

Focusing on Workspace

"The [couple's] workspaces were considered to be as important [as] their main living spaces and were designed for specific tasks. Judith's weaving studio, in particular, became an architectural focal point of the house. The studio showcases the work of local craftspeople, but it also reflects our design intention to have the house open itself to the outside, as well as provide private interior spaces. The main floor of the studio, which houses a big loom and a textile storage wall, is visible as one approaches the house, and it is very open to the outdoors."

—Scott Neeley,
Scott Neeley & Associates Architecture

■ Like many of the rooms in Judith and David's new home, the weaving studio features wood used from their land. A salvaged cedar trunk was fashioned into a newel and stair railing.

cedar newel and railing are in themselves works of art. The second-floor loft, up a short flight of steps, contains Judith's library. Though the studio faces east, northern light floods the space through French doors. Even more natural light infiltrates the studio when it streams in from the small, side porch where Judith steps out for a breath of fresh air.

Retired from academia and the corporate world, David now runs a tree farm from his office and study, which is tucked away behind the living-room fireplace and overlooks stands of hardwood trees. The room is lined with bookcases and floored with oak cut on the property.

Both workspaces are in the wing with the living spaces—Judith's studio in front of the house, David's study at the back—illustrating how a couple can live and work separately but together while pursuing their passions.

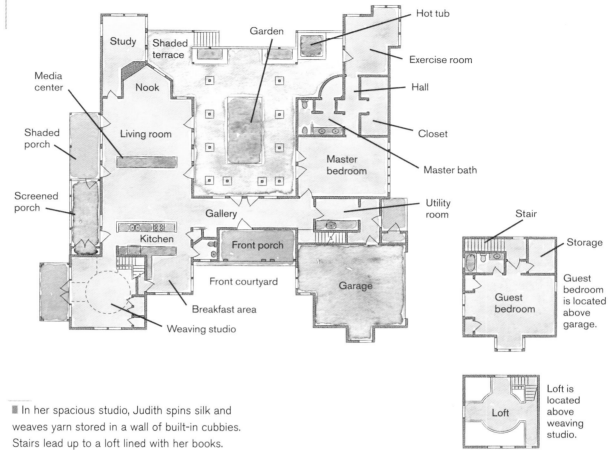

Study

Shaded terrace

Garden

Hot tub

Exercise room

Media center

Nook

Hall

Shaded porch

Living room

Closet

Screened porch

Master bedroom

Master bath

Gallery

Utility room

Kitchen

Front porch

Stair

Storage

Front courtyard

Garage

Guest bedroom

Guest bedroom is located above garage.

Breakfast area

Weaving studio

Loft

Loft is located above weaving studio.

SECOND FLOOR

■ In her spacious studio, Judith spins silk and weaves yarn stored in a wall of built-in cubbies. Stairs lead up to a loft lined with her books.

Simulating a Rural Past

The couple ensured the integrity of their farmhouse design, however contemporary it might be, by using local materials, such as hardwood grown and harvested on the property. Elsewhere, new materials simulate a rural past. The roofing, for instance, is faded red hexagonal shingle, an antiquated-looking product that is manufactured from a cement-fiber compound.

The couple also involved the local arts and crafts community, of which they had become a part of over the years, by hiring local craftspeople to help in the design of the house. A furniture maker and friend made the front door, sideboard, mantel, and studio staircase from local walnut and the divider cabinets from maple. Another craftsperson, who restores cathedral windows, designed and installed the three stained-glass windows in the house. Finally, a local mason built the Rumsford fireplace.

■ The second-floor studio loft, with a hand-crafted railing made from cedar grown on the property, is the place for the artist's favorite art and sewing books. The loft window, inspired by a Frank Lloyd Wright design, is one of three such windows in the house.

Looking from the dining room to the kitchen, a notched divider covered in tongue-and-groove boards separates the rooms. The spaces let air and light pass through the rooms.

Removing Physical Obstacles

The couple thoroughly implemented their design ideas, planning for the present as well as the future. Aside from the studio loft and guest room over the garage, there are no stairs in the house. Doorways measure 3 feet wide (compared with the standard door measurement of 2 feet 6 inches wide), and the master bath includes a shower that accommodates a wheelchair.

In the event the couple needs full-time care in the future, the exercise room off the master bedroom can convert into a caretaker's bedroom. Or, for more privacy, there's the garage apartment or the restored cabin located 1,000 feet away.

For now, however, it's just the two of them—at home with one another and with the art and work that continue to sustain them.

The living room's 14-foot-high ceiling is uplit with small spots on the cross beams, while low-voltage cable lights provide accent lighting below. The broad room divider looks like a handsome piece of furniture, while concealing the television and other entertainment paraphernalia.

The central courtyard is paved with low-maintenance, colored concrete. The pergola is covered with wisteria, honeysuckle, morning glory, and Carolina jasmine to partially shade the windows on the walkway from the summer sun.

This angled fireplace nook at the far end of the living room creates a focal point—and a private space for the couple—in an otherwise open, rectilinear room. The mantel, which melds into the bookcases, is made from the same walnut trees as the front door, sideboard, and kitchen cabinets.

The House They Always Wanted

"THE HOUSE WE ONCE LIVED IN WAS A COLLECTION OF COMPARTMENTALIZED, ISOLATED ROOMS. WE WANTED AN OPEN HOUSE DESIGNED AROUND MULTIPLE-USE ROOMS THAT WE WOULD USE FREQUENTLY. THE LIVING ROOM HAD TO BE AN INFORMAL PLACE, NOT A SPACE WHERE WE'D ONLY SIT IN DURING FORMAL OCCASIONS."

—DAVID, HOMEOWNER

A NEW OLD-WORLD HOUSE

Northwest Montana

From the rear terrace, the Hartmans' house overlooks stands of 150-year-old pine trees and a crystal-clear lake. The terrace combines an unusual mix of materials: wood construction, wrought-iron railings, and massive, stucco-covered concrete piers that echo the classical style of the rest of the house.

Sometimes, a couple's travels and life experience informs the design of a house more than a popular style or an architect's vision. Perhaps it is true that the more one has lived, the more one knows how to live.

Rick and Pauline Hartman always knew they would retire one day to a remote part of an extreme northwest section of Montana. In 1995, they purchased a six-acre cherry orchard, referred to by the locals as "Bear-dancer," and planned to move into the small house that was already on the property.

Soon after buying the property, Rick faced a traumatic medical scare; it was one that he would survive, but the incident changed their plans. The couple decided to build the house of their dreams on the site and hired architect Anne Olson to design one that would remind them of their extensive trips to Ireland and France.

Along with flea-market finds the couple brought back from their trips, Rick and Pauline also developed a love for the timeless, enduring qualities of the old, country manor houses they explored overseas. Anne designed the house so that the couple could enjoy their new life to the fullest. The house addresses the couple's passions: It is a mix of Irish, English, and French manor-house styles; it takes advantage of the views of the Montana countryside; and it's built for entertaining.

Looking more like the interior of a hundred-year-old European manor than a new house in the wilds of Montana, thick plaster walls and a delicate wrought-iron railing frame the grand staircase to the owner's master bedroom suite.

The House They Always Wanted

"WHEN YOU FACE SOMETHING THAT THREATENS YOUR EXISTENCE, YOU LEARN TO LIVE LIFE TO THE FULLEST, AND WE WANTED A HOUSE DESIGNED TO REFLECT THAT. WE WANTED IT TO HAVE THE DESIGN OF AN OLD WORLD, EUROPEAN-STYLE HOUSE MADE OF STONE AND THICK PLASTER. BUT WE WANTED A HOUSE THAT WAS LUXURIOUS BECAUSE WE WANT OUR GUESTS TO FEEL PAMPERED."

—PAULINE HARTMAN, HOMEOWNER

A European-Inspired Facade

When the Hartmans first met with Anne, Pauline drew her dream home on a napkin. The drawing was of a plain rectangle bookended with large fireplaces, like the type she saw during her European travels. Pauline asked Anne to make everything in the house look old and like stone.

To achieve the look of stone, stucco was hand-troweled over chicken wire affixed to the exterior wood lathing. The homeowners were even more delighted when the builder told them that the stucco would eventually crack. For an extra Old World touch, ivy now climbs the walls, clinging to the cracks in the stucco.

To the otherwise plain facade, precast concrete replicas of classic ornamental elements were added around the doorway and windows. Shield-shaped keystones—the decorative elements at the top of the arches—were inspired by Pauline's memories of Europe and her imagination. These small but powerful details establish the sensibility and frame of European reference for the whole house.

▌ An old fruit-picker's cabin on the property was converted into a charming, private guest house complete with a deck overlooking the lake.

The drama and embellishment of the recessed entry sets the stage for a house devoted to the art of entertaining. The arches, niches, ornamental precast concrete, and delicate wrought ironwork capture the European flavor the couple experienced during their travels. The 39-inch-high lanterns are crafted from solid copper, another Old World detail that makes this house unique.

The homeowners found this 100-year-old double door, made of sandalwood and walnut, in an architectural salvage store in Denver. Behind the wrought-iron details are operable hinged windows.

A Romantic Interior

The look of stone continues inside the house. The interior walls were made to resemble stone using the same hand-applied plaster method used on the exterior. As the light changes in the house so does the color of the walls. An ocher pigment mixed into the third and final layer of plaster causes the color of the walls to change throughout the day from lemon to gold to green to chalky white.

Guests enter the house through the baronial dining room. Influenced by Irish manor houses, the room has a fireplace and is also lit by a 20-candle candelabra. The travertine stone floors are the kind frequently found in old manor houses.

Like the lobby of a fine, family-owned European hotel, the living room feels welcoming. Tall windows showcasing a canopy of trees keep the room, with its 24-foot-high ceiling, from feeling cold and stark.

The walls are 12 inches thick in places to replicate the sense of the weight and permanence of ancient stone buildings. The thick plasterwork also enabled the architect to design arches and niches throughout the house. Aside from breaking up the vast expanses of stonelike, interior walls, the niches—another Old World touch—showcase art objects and photographs without cluttering the pure form of the interior spaces, as cabinets or bookcases would.

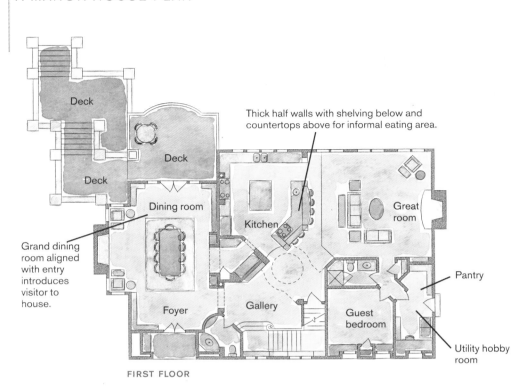

Thick half walls with shelving below and countertops above for informal eating area.

Deck

Deck

Deck

Dining room

Kitchen

Great room

Grand dining room aligned with entry introduces visitor to house.

Pantry

Foyer

Gallery

Guest bedroom

Utility hobby room

FIRST FLOOR

Rooms with a View

The architect positioned all of the rooms in the house to get the best views of the landscape, including pine trees, fruit trees, and a lake. The dining-room and living-room ceilings are 24 feet high to let in as much of the view as possible. The home's wide-open plan lets the homeowners see the views from just about anywhere they stand in the house. In fact, the two-story windows in both public rooms create living murals, eliminating the need to hang wall art.

The outside views inspired the design of the second-floor master suite. The master bedroom is a loft space separated from the staircase and master bath by a bridge. The bedroom and the bridge—which is like an indoor balcony—look over the living room and share the views and natural light coming in from the oversize windows. A large balcony off another side of the bedroom overlooks the dining room and its two-story views. "Our bedroom makes us feel like we are sleeping in a tree house," Pauline says. "We're as close as we can get to being in the tops of these towering old pines."

■ The chef never feels cooped up in this kitchen, where the workspace counter doubles as an entertainment bar for the adjoining living room. With no overhead cabinets in the way, Rick can see the view of trees and water while creating a feast.

BREAKING THE RULES

Although the Hartmans' house has an open floor plan—one of the design characteristics of the new empty-nester house—the way the space is used breaks a few empty-nester rules. While many empty nesters opt for a first-floor bedroom, this master suite is accessed by a steep flight of stairs. In addition, it is located directly over the grandchildren's guest room, where the couple can revel in the joyful sounds of their little visitors. The master bedroom is also open—like a loft—on two sides, exposing it to the living room where an abundance of natural light streams in through the two-story windows. In this way, the master bedroom becomes part of the living space rather than sheltered away at the back of the house.

■ Beyond the knee-wall, the second-floor master bedroom opens up into the living room. From the bedroom, the couple can see outdoors through the living room windows.

SECOND FLOOR

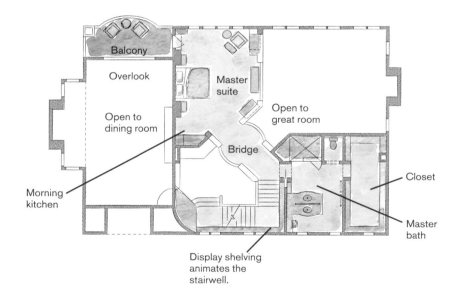

■ Plaster walls that are 8 inches to 12 inches thick give the house a timeless, enduring quality and echo the construction of the stone manors the couple fell in love with during their travels.

A Luxury Hotel

Rick and Pauline's home feels like a small, family-owned European hotel that pampers dinner guests and welcomes them to stay the night. It also pampers the owners: A "morning kitchen" in the master-bedroom suite contains a small refrigerator, sink, microwave, and coffeemaker.

The first room inside a house often says a lot about how the homeowners feel about greeting their guests. Some front entrances open into claustrophobic hallways, ceremonial living rooms, or cluttered family rooms that need straightening up before the guests arrive. Rick and Pauline wanted their entry to be a formal, elegant expression of their warm hospitality.

The large, 16-foot-wide by 35-foot-long foyer opens directly to the formidable, 450-square-foot dining room. Spaces this lofty can sometimes feel spare and cold, but a 6-foot-high fireplace, a soft color palette, and lush views of the woods and the water make the room feel welcoming.

Hand-plastered surfaces, three layers thick, create sculpted walls and ceilings that need no extra ornamentation. Above the gallery, on the second-floor bridge, a balcony becomes part of the theater of the house.

A Passion for Entertaining

The Hartmans' eagerness to pamper their guests is also articulated in the kitchen, which serves as Rick's stage. The professionally outfitted kitchen is equipped with two sinks, two ovens, warming drawers, an eight-burner cooktop, a Sub-Zero® refrigerator, and a slate and stainless-steel island. Unlike kitchens tucked into a rear corner of a house, this space is the heart of the house, commanding a large section of the central part of the floor plan.

After dinner, guests retire to one of two separate buildings on the property, which includes the former main house located 100 yards away and a restored cabin once used in the 1880s as a fishing base camp and then later as a bunkhouse for fruit pickers. It's just the kind of informal, romantic atmosphere the couple desired when they designed the house they always wanted for themselves.

A RETREAT FAR FROM HOME

San Miguel de Allende, Mexico

CATHI AND STEVEN HOUSE, both architects, made it a point to travel the world, often globe-hopping for their San Francisco–based architectural firm. It was one trip to Mexico that led them to the ideal place where they would start their new lives.

Cathi fell in love with the old, sleepy village of San Miguel de Allende while on a business trip. The village, which dates back to 1542, has cobblestone streets, walled gardens, and courtyards and attracts a community of artisans who live there year round. She soon returned with her husband, Steven, and the couple vacationed there every year, as the colonial Mexican village gradually became their retreat. Ten years after they discovered the village, the couple bought a lot near the center of town on which they built their dream getaway.

Designed in the mid-1990s around a courtyard, architectural studio, and crafts workspace, the main house was the refuge of their dreams. But as they began sharing this paradise with family and friends, the couple quickly found their work and peace of mind disrupted. The solution was to build a new house three doors away to accommodate guests. Now, their retreat consists of a main house the couple uses for work and sleep and a guest house for entertaining.

■ Located four blocks from the center of town, time seems to stand still on this quiet street of old villas where one couple built their retreat. A 100-year-old carpenter's bench, scarred by hammer and saw marks (facing page), was scribed and framed by Francisco Caballero, a carpenter from the village, then turned into an 11-foot-long dinner table.

■ The entry courtyard seems to change color throughout the day. Here, the underside of the staircase, next to a wet bar and towering column, resembles an inverted, abstract sculpture of steps.

A Courtyard Escape

The 2,000-square-foot guest house, built five years after the main house, is hidden from the street behind a two-story concrete wall. The design of the guest house consists of several indoor/outdoor spaces that orient themselves around an inner courtyard. Each room on the first floor has access to the central courtyard as well as limited access to private outdoor spaces. The master bedroom, surrounded by a semicircle of burgundy-colored columns, also opens into the courtyard and to a private garden.

The guest house looks like an architectural sculpture, designed to let the Mexican sun carve out patterns of light and shadow on the concrete, tile, and wood surfaces. The true art of the design of the guest house comes from the way the rooms glow when sunlight is funneled inside during most of the day. Openings in the walls are placed high and next to textured surfaces so that when the fierce Mexican sun streams inside, it is diffused onto the rough surfaces. As the light shifts during the day, the lime-washed walls and stairs seem to change colors.

Unlike houses designed in cooler climates, this tropical guest house isn't the right place for sunrooms or greenhouse windows. In the shade of the pomegranate tree, the courtyard is a place to escape from the sun and stay cool.

RESPECTING THE NEIGHBORHOOD

Cathi and Steven realized that it would take some social finesse to build a house in a foreign land. Building in another country, and within a different culture, can be unsettling for the neighbors, especially when it's in a historic town where change comes slowly.

Acknowledging this, the couple wanted their neighbors to know they respected the neighborhood and the local traditions. "We went into the neighborhood with the utmost respect," Cathi says. "Most of our neighbors were born and raised here. We knocked on doors before we bought the site to make sure no one had any negative feelings about us moving in."

The couple also studied the region's architecture and craft traditions and employed local craftspeople in order to add the special, regional details that help the main house and guest house fit in with the landscape of the town.

■ Local blacksmiths forged the wrought-iron railings, which cast shifting shadows all day. The play of sun across the roof and courtyard was used as a design element in the house.

Life in this house revolves around the courtyard, a refuge from the street below and from the intense Mexican sun. Drains located under the cool-to-the-touch paving stones catch and store water collected from the tropical rains.

Eight concrete columns, rubbed smooth by hand, inscribe the semicircular master bedroom, which is a temple of solitude for the homeowners' guests. Beyond the columns is a door to the courtyard, followed by a second door out to a private garden.

The House We Always Wanted

"AFTER YEARS OF TRAVELING, WE WANTED A PLACE THAT WAS OURS AND THAT WOULD EMBRACE US THE MOMENT WE WALKED IN. THE COURTYARD HOUSES PROVIDE A PROTECTIVE, CALMING ATMOSPHERE. EVERYTHING ABOUT THE HOUSES REPRESENTS OUR LIVES AND OUR SOULS. WE WANTED TO CREATE AN INTERIOR WORLD WITH A SENSE OF CONNECTION TO THE OUTER WORLD WITHOUT LETTING IT IN AND WITHOUT BARRICADING OURSELVES FROM THE OUTSIDE. THE GOVERNING PRINCIPLE HERE WAS TO CHOREOGRAPH THESE SPACES FOR OUR EVERYDAY MOVEMENTS."

—CATHI HOUSE,
HOMEOWNER AND ARCHITECT

Mexican Influences

The courtyard is paved in a mosaic of smooth river stones depicting an ancient Mayan pictograph, but that's just one of many cultural influences found throughout the guest house.

Large openings in the concrete walls reveal the influence of contemporary Mexican architect Louis Barragan, who experimented with geometric forms and windows that varied wildly in size. The use of stone floors, twisting concrete staircases, and intricate wrought-iron railings are also ubiquitous to the region. The vibrant colors of the concrete that appear throughout the house are custom mixes of local lime washes—colors not normally found in North America, such as the deep cobalt blue with its purplish cast, the cool mint and sage greens, and the refreshing mango orange.

OPEN TO THE OUTDOORS

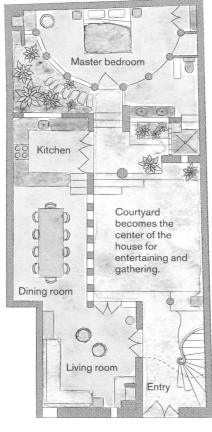

Master bedroom

Kitchen

Courtyard becomes the center of the house for entertaining and gathering.

Dining room

Living room

Entry

FIRST FLOOR

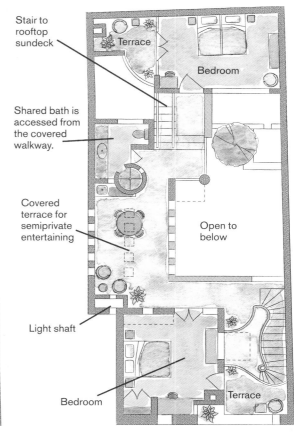

Stair to rooftop sundeck

Shared bath is accessed from the covered walkway.

Covered terrace for semiprivate entertaining

Light shaft

Terrace

Bedroom

Open to below

Bedroom

Terrace

SECOND FLOOR

■ Most homes in Mexico are centered around an inner courtyard. Steven and Cathi's house honors the presence of a 200-year-old pomegranate tree, shown in the background. The courtyard floor is a mosaic of muted river stones, with a design based on ancient Mayan pictographs.

In the entry courtyard, the railing of the lime-washed staircase is capped with hand-polished, mint-green concrete.

A Handmade House

Cathi and Steven could have loaded a container of building materials from the States—a common practice among Americans building abroad. But San Miguel de Allende is known for superb local materials, timeless methods of construction, and skilled craftspeople. The couple asked local artisans to make by hand nearly every design element in the house, from the wrought-iron railings and glass door frames and handles to the cabinetry and concrete surfaces and finishes.

This one-of-a-kind house incorporates the riches of the local terrain and the talents of the neighboring artisans. The floors of the courtyard and the front-door surround are made of slate removed from a site with a pick and carted down from the mountains on burros. The stones for other parts of the courtyard's mosaic floors, handpicked by the contractor's crew from a nearby riverbed, were carried back to the house in sacks, a common building practice in Mexico.

The vibrantly colored bathroom on the second floor has a tall, slit window that looks onto the terrace above the courtyard.

■ A terrace off the second-floor bedroom is a gallery of bold geometrical shapes and exotic colors, from the large cylinder that serves as an outer wall of an interior shower to the rectangular balcony posts. The staggered steps in the background lead up to a rooftop terrace. Each terrace has a wet bar, a creature comfort that makes this retreat a complete oasis.

▌ Adorned with intricate ironwork, a second-floor bedroom terrace catches morning light from the rooftop above and the courtyard below. Interior outdoor spaces like these are frequently found around town.

▌ A glass door and transom in the living room were made by a local blacksmith and finished on-site by an itinerant glazier. In the outer entry hallway, the winding staircase is concrete, as is the hearth in the room. The concrete was lime-washed and polished by hand—a local material and traditional method that the homeowners respected and wanted to use throughout their home. To the right of the mantel, a glass-block window peeks out to the street at a child's eye level.

The workers' dedication to their crafts turned wood and stone into objects of art. The crew spent days mixing oxides and lime and rubbing the concrete railings and columns by hand. A carpenter from the neighborhood built the front door and cabinets, then scribed (marked and cut to fit) new wood around an old, unevenly edged carpenter's bench to create an 11-foot-long table for the dining room. A local blacksmith forged the delicate wrought-iron railings as well as the door and window frames that counterpoint the thick concrete used throughout the house on floors, steps, and walls. Every inch of the guest house is infused with regional color and bold creativity.

On the ruins of an old structure, Cathi and Steven built a modern interpretation of the traditional courtyard plan indigenous to Mexico. In doing so, the couple is able to experience, and comfortably share with friends and family, the exotic land they fell in love with so long ago.

▌ The rooftop terrace looks back to Steven and Cathi's studio, located three town houses away from the guest residence. Over the years, the colonial Mexican village has become their physical, professional, and spiritual retreat.

HARVESTING THE LAND

Portland, Oregon

Whited Ben and Sandy's children were all out of the house, the couple turned their attention to living a simplified, renewed life. Ben retired from his sales job and the two of them moved from their large family home to a 60-acre orchard south of Portland, where they planned to harvest chestnuts for sale to gourmet and health-food stores. But they also came to the Willamette Valley for the views.

The couple wanted a new house that would hug the land and capture panoramic views. Having acquired a degree of architectural awareness over the years, they also wanted a house constructed of high-quality materials and designed to bring family members together without sacrificing privacy. The couple hired architect Richard Brown to design the 2,800-square-foot retirement house that sits as unobtrusively on the land as a stand of trees. Brown went about achieving these ends through imaginative means, and in ways that bring the traditional Northwest style into the 21st century.

Capturing All Views

Ben and Sandy took six years getting to know the land they bought before building their house. They walked through the land's contours, up and down the hills,

■ Exposed rafter tails and tongue-and-groove boards in the roof overhang are Craftsman-style characteristics that give the house a Northwest flavor. The rooms of the house are angled at 60 degrees on the lower level and 90 degrees on top in order to take in the full sweep of orchards, meadows, and mountains.

■ Life in this retirement house centers around the kitchen, which flows into the family room. Maple and fir cabinets are finished with easy-to-maintain poured-in-place concrete countertops. Free of upper cabinets, the kitchen windows frame sweeping views of farmland and mountains.

■ In the living room, a Rumsford fireplace sits in an alcove of Douglas fir bookcases. The curved ceiling breaks up the verticality of the bookcases.

■ ARCHITECT'S NOTES

A Rare Design Collaboration

To help blend the house into the landscape, John David Forsgren, a designer who specializes in finishes, worked with architect Richard Brown to create the nature-inspired palette of colors used inside and outside each structure. "This type of collaboration means that the clients end up with a cohesive house. They won't get idea 'A' on the exterior and idea 'B' on the interior," John explains.

The surrounding countryside inspired John to create the palette of painted, dark exterior tones. The deep blue-green of the main house resembles the color of the nearby forest of fir and oaks. The deep blue guest house mirrors the hues of the hills in the background, and the grayish purple of the garage blends in with a sky that often has a purplish cast.

John chose nine soothing shades of green for the interior as a way to bring nature inside. The green palette also contrasts with the natural-wood cabinets and trim used throughout the house.

HUGGING THE LAND

Garage

Main house

Guest cabin

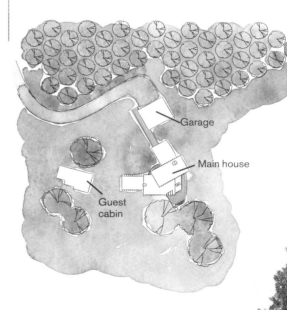

■ The guest wing of the main house looks out to a leafy garden and detached guest house, forming a secluded compound far from the owners' master suite.

through the meadows that roll down to groves of chestnut, oak, and evergreen trees, and took in the views of Mount Hood.

They chose a gently sloping hilltop on which to construct the main house because it offered the largest variety of vistas. After the site for the house was chosen, it became clear that the house would be designed to maximize the views and to help the homeowners best experience the landscape.

The main house is comprised of two first-floor wings, each with curved outer walls to take advantage of panoramic views of the

■ The back door of a farmhouse, even a contemporary one like this, functions as the main entrance. The trellised path, covered with narrow strips of shower-door glass, leads visitors from the parking area to the door; it also ties the garage to the house. Directly inside the door is the home office, where Ben and Sandy pursue a retirement career of harvesting chestnuts.

The living room (foreground) flows uninterrupted into an ample entry and stairway hall, then into the dining room, at right. The columns frame the stairs, rather than support the ceiling. Doors at the top of the stairs seal off the master-bedroom suite from the downstairs living areas.

The radiant-heated concrete floor in the dining room and hallway was poured in place and finely troweled. The flooring warms up the feet, and the matte-black finish is easy on the eye because it softly contrasts with the natural woods, pale-colored walls, and expanses of glass around the house.

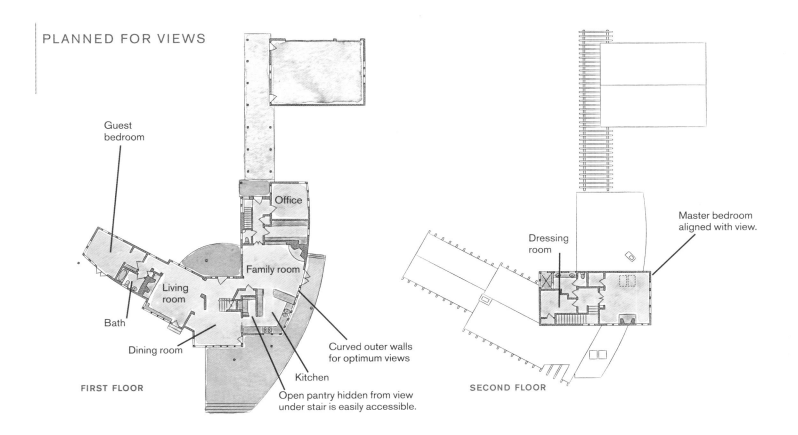

FIRST FLOOR

Guest bedroom

Office

Family room

Living room

Bath

Dining room

Kitchen

Curved outer walls for optimum views

Open pantry hidden from view under stair is easily accessible.

SECOND FLOOR

Master bedroom aligned with view.

Dressing room

meadows, woods, and distant mountain. The second floor sits balanced on top of the lower wings. The bedroom is angled so it is in direct sight of Mount Hood, a mountain located 50 miles from the house.

Fifty feet away from the main house sits the guest quarters—a two-story, 500-square-foot structure with two bedrooms, one bath, kitchen, and living room with fireplace. A third building, containing a garage and workshop, is also separate from the house but connected by a 55-foot trellis. The distance between buildings opens this side of the house up so that light, air, and views can permeate the interiors.

A Modern Floor Plan

Indoors, all the public rooms pivot off the front-entry vestibule and flow into one another. This modern arrangement—rooms that open up into one another—make a home appropriate for entertaining.

The major factor influencing the design of the floor plan was a desire to bring a large family together for weekends, holidays, and vacations, without sacrificing privacy—or sanity. It was a desire mixed with the need to accommodate four children and eight grandchildren, all of whom live out of state.

The extensive use of Douglas fir in the kitchen (foreground) and family room warms up the look of the open space.

The 15-foot-wide by 18-foot-long master bedroom feels like a private, luxurious hotel suite well removed from the often crowded public spaces below. Two-foot-wide columns, which are deep enough to provide space for inset book-cases on both sides, define the doorway and create a cozy corner study, at left.

The second-floor master bed-room features a cathedral ceiling of exposed rafters, tongue-and-groove planking, skylights, and windows with fixed transoms angled up to the gabled ridge. Since Ben and Sandy have the floor to themselves, there's no need for privacy; wide French doors of Douglas fir and glass lead to the master bath and a walk-through closet and dress-ing room.

At the same time, however, the layout provides freedom and privacy. The single guest room in the main house, for example, is located at the west end of the structure—close, but not too close, to the master bedroom suite. It's buffered from the large social space—the living room—by a laundry room and a bathroom that serves the adjoining space. The juxtaposition makes the guest room into a semiprivate suite. Since this end of the house does not have prime views (it faces the nearest neighbor and an outbuilding on the property), fewer windows are necessary, resulting in more privacy for visitors.

Ben and Sandy are free to get away to the opposite end of the main house, through closed doors and up the stairs to their 270-square-foot master-bedroom suite high above the fray on the second floor. For faster, shorter getaways without leaving the house, the couple can retreat into the home office, off the back hallway, or down to the basement, where there are workbenches and a wine cellar—a handy space to have during long family visits.

The House They Always Wanted

"WE'VE BEEN BUILDING A HOUSE IN OUR MINDS FOR YEARS. WHEN WE WERE IN COLLEGE, WE WOULD LOOK AT FRANK LLOYD WRIGHT HOUSES TOGETHER, SO WE WERE LEANING TOWARD A CONTEMPORARY STYLE. BUT WE DIDN'T WANT IT TO BE A BLIGHT ON THE LAND. WE WANTED A HOUSE THAT COMPLIMENTED THE SURROUNDINGS."

—BEN AND SANDY, HOMEOWNERS

One reason the couple moved to the area was to enjoy the sweeping views of the land, seen here from the deck off the dining room.

Directory of Architects and Designers

THE GEOMETRY OF TWO LIVES (p. 48)
Peter Pfau, AIA
Pfau Architecture Ltd.
630 Third St., Ste. 200
San Francisco CA 94017
415-908-6408
www.pfauarchitecture.com

REFINING THE RANCH (p. 88)
Buzz Yudell, FAIA
Moore Ruble Yudell Architects & Planners
933 Pico Blvd.
Santa Monica, CA 90405
310-450-1400
www.mryarchitects.com

A HIP RETIREMENT HAVEN (p. 24)
Cathleen Quandt
Sheahan + Quandt Architecture
2413-C Fifth St.
Berkeley, CA 94710
510-849-3934
www.sheahan-quandt.com

Cheng Design
2808 Pablo Ave.
Berkeley, CA 94702
510-849-3272
www.chengdesign.com
interior design: Fu-Tung Cheng

TOGETHER ON THE RIVER (p. 58)
Mark McInturff, FAIA
McInturff Architects
4220 Leeward Pl.
Bethesda, MD 20816
301-229-3705
www.mcinturffarchitects.com
design associate: Megan Walsh, AIA

FIELD OF DREAMS (p. 98)
Dan Wheeler, AIA
Wheeler Kearns Architects
417 S. Dearborn St.
Chicago, IL 60605
312-939-7787
www.wkarch.com
interior design: Cynthia Ruhaak

AT HOME ON THE RANGE (p. 32)
Mell Lawrence, AIA
Mell Lawrence Architects
913 W. Gibson St.
Austin, TX 78704
512-441-4669
www.architecturalpolka.com
interior design: Cindy Severson Studio
512-474-2684

A SHIPSHAPE HOUSE FOR TWO (p. 68)
Philip Christofides, AIA
Arellano-Christofides Architects
1402 3rd Ave., Ste. 925
Seattle, WA 98101
206-623-0511
www.arellano-christofides.com

AN OLD COTTAGE MADE NEW (p. 108)
James Estes
Estes/Twombly Architects, Inc.
79 Thames St.
Newport, RI 02840
401-846-3336
www.estestwombly.com

IN THE COMPANY OF FRIENDS (p. 40)
Laura Hartman
Fernau & Hartman
2512 Ninth St. #2
Berkeley, CA 94710
510-848-4480
www.fernauhartman.com

A COUPLE'S ISLAND LODGE (p. 78)
Geoffrey T. Prentiss
Prentiss Architects, Inc.
224 W. Galer St., Ste. A
Seattle, WA 98119
206-283-9930
www.prentissarch.com

A NEST FOR THE FUTURE (p. 118)
Robert Orr, AIA
Robert Orr & Associates
441 Chapel St.
New Haven, CT 06511
203-777-3387
www.robertorr.com
interior design: Robert and Carol Orr

AN ADDITION FOR TWO OR MORE (p. 126)
Stephen Dynia, AIA

Stephen Dynia Architects
1135 Maple Way
Jackson, WY 83001
307-733-3766
dyniaarchitects.com

DESIGNED WITH OFFSPRING IN MIND (p. 136)
Mark Simon, FAIA

Centerbrook Architects and Planners
67 Main St.
Centerbrook, CT 06409
860-767-0175
www.centerbrook.com

A MODERN DESERT HOME (p. 144)
Eddie Jones

Jones Studio
4450 N 12th St.
Phoenix, AZ 85014
602-264-2941
www.jonesstudioinc.com

A FAMILY COMPOUND SPREADS OUT (p. 154)
Mark Hutker

Mark Hutker and Associates Architects
P.O. Box 2347
Tisbury Market Pl.
Beach Rd.
Vineyard Haven, MA 02568
508-693-3344
www.hutkerarchitects.com

FROM CRAMPED TO COMFORTABLE (p. 164)
John Malick

John Malick & Associates
195 Park Ave.
Ste. 102
Emeryville, CA 94608
510-595-8042
www.jmalick.com

TIME FOR A CHANGE (p. 174)
Craig Saunders, AIA

Du Bose Associates, Inc. Architects
49 Woodland St.
Hartford, CT 06105
860-249-9387
www.dbarch.com
designer: Helen Theurkauf
Theurkauf & Company
860-633-2420

A WEAVER AND WOODCUTTER'S REFUGE (p. 182)
Scott Neeley

Scott Neeley & Associates Architecture
515 G St.
Davis, CA 95616
scott@neeleyarchitect.com
in association with:
Clearscapes, PA
311 W. Martin St.
Raleigh, NC 27601
919-821-2775

A NEW OLD-WORLD HOUSE (p. 190)
Anne Olson

Olson Architecture, Inc.
P.O. Box 1024
Niwot, CO 80544
303-652-2668
aolson@boulder.net

A RETREAT FAR FROM HOME (p. 198)
Cathi House

House + House Architects
1499 Washington St.
San Francisco, CA 94109
415-474-2112
house@ix.netcom.com
interior design:
Cathi and Steven House

HARVESTING THE LAND (p. 208)
Richard Brown, AIA, LLP

Richard Brown Architects
239 NW 13th St., Rm. 305
Portland, OR 97209
503-223-4957
rbarch@europa.com
interior design: John David Forsgren